the Sacred Impulse

JAMES CONLON

the Sacred Impulse

A Planetary Spirituality of Heart and Fire

A Crossroad Book
The Crossroad Publishing Company
New York

The Crossroad Publishing Company
370 Lexington Avenue, New York, NY 10017

Printed in the United States of America

Library of Congress Cataloging-in-Publication Data
Conlon, James, 1936-
    The sacred impulse : A planetary spirituality of heart and fire /
by James Conlon.
      p. cm.
    ISBN 0-8245-1865-9
    1. Spiritual life. 2. Human ecology – Religious life. I. Title.
BL624 .C663 2000
291.4′4–dc21

00-008945

1 2 3 4 5 6 7 8 9 10   06 05 04 03 02 01 00

Contents

Foreword
by Diarmuid O'Murchu

Some books leave an enduring impact. They touch the heart and fire the imagination. For me one such book was Jim Conlon's first work, *Geo-Justice*, a seminal work highlighting the fact that our commitment to justice is seriously deficient if we ignore or bypass the planet we inhabit and the cosmos to which we belong. It is an urgent and timely message that has scarcely been heard by the religious or political leaders of our time.

In *The Sacred Impulse*, Jim returns afresh to the theme of geo-justice, but this time couched within a spiritual context that adds profundity and verve to his enduring passion. Justice without spirituality can easily lead to a harshness and cynicism that undermines true liberation. The issues — especially on a global scale — are so vast and complex that we are often left with an overwhelming sense of powerlessness. On the other hand, spirituality without a practical commitment to justice can easily become escapist and blasphemous as we expect God to work some divine miracle to rectify the wrongs committed by us human beings.

Jim combines the spiritual search and the justice calling within his passionate commitment to the unfolding of the New Creation Story. The vision, and some of its practical applications, are succinctly outlined in two key passages:

> A justice that flows from the New Story will provide us with a fresh sense of equity among self, others, and creation. A re-

newed view of justice will foster in each of us a deep intention to carry out the historical mission to which we are called, to participate in the great transitions taking place in our time, to restore creation to its pristine beauty, and to restructure society to a greater degree of mutuality and magnificence.

Our spiritual journey is evolutionary, holistic, and mystical. ... The spiritual journey leads to liberation, feminism, a new economics, participatory politics, and ecological sensitivity. ... A spirituality that flows out of the New Story and that is deeply integrated into the practice of justice-making fosters hope and supports creativity.

What transpires from this timely work is a fresh sense of *vocation,* one that rightly challenges Joanna Macy's perception that ours is a "vocationless culture." The problem is that we have overspiritualized the concept of vocation, portraying a holier-than-thou image that is inconceivable apart from the context of church or formal religion.

In his capacity as director of the Sophia Center, Jim knows from daily experience that many people today are fired with a genuine sense of vocation, one that tends to focus on the critical questions of our *world* and not on the preoccupying questions of church or religion.

Indeed, it is for these very people — the searching souls of our time — that *The Sacred Impulse* can provide, not just an inspiring read, but substantial spiritual nourishment to sustain perseverance and hope as we strive to bring about a more just and wholesome universe.

Acknowledgments

To the students, faculty, staff, and advisory council of Sophia Center, whose response to their own prompting has energized this work.

To Marilyn Goddard, Mary Tuchscherer, and Anastasia MacDonald, whose good work and support have made the preparation of these pages possible.

To Joan LaFlamme and Paul Weisser, who worked closely with me.

To all the prophetic people whose sacred impulses have given inspiration and whose words are contained in the text.

To the mystery and magnificence of the universe, whose undiminished flame of beauty is the source of all energy and new life.

Introduction

Early Christian philosophers operated on a credo of "see, judge, and act," but we have altered that structure. We as Western Christians tend to go into a situation and judge: We don't do the seeing. Seeing is all about the contemplative aspect of spirituality which leads to a deep, perceptive sense of insight and understanding. —DIARMUID O'MURCHU

The Sacred Impulse is written for a "generation of seekers" who are searching for a spirituality to guide, inspire, and energize their lives. Each chapter is designed to evoke those sacred impulses that find inspiration in and through the heart and fire of our lives.

Chapter 1, "Our Vocational Destiny," invites us to develop a grand vision to foster new levels of depth and understanding in regard to our cities, historical figures, and those sacred places on the planet where we lived as children and where we continue to listen to the voice of vocation.

Chapter 2, "The New Story," reflects on the New Creation Story as a new, hope-filled context for our lives — a place to remember our origins, ponder the present, and celebrate the future.

Chapter 3, "A Dynamic Relationship," develops a dynamic integration of the New Creation Story and the story of geo-justice. We are guided in our historical mission as our actions in the world become aligned to the dynamics of the universe.

Chapter 4, "The Spiritual Journey," contributes to a fresh comprehension of a planetary spirituality that celebrates the unfolding story of Earth, the creative impulse of art, and the profound experience of the spirit that moves deep within and outward toward transformation.

Chapter 5, "Recognizing Our Origins," names primary archetypal Christian symbols, energetic patterns that reside deep in the psyche and that today represent a new synthesis of the wisdom that is available to us from science, indigenous peoples, women, and classical traditions.

Chapter 6, "A Story of Hope," offers an emerging vision of a planetary spirituality that will guide and energize our lives as we embark on a journey that is personal, communal, and cosmic — a journey that invites us into the future with fresh momentum and hope.

The sacred impulse is a clarion call to reciprocity as we weave together a tapestry of interdependence to enhance the landscape of our souls and quilt a web of compassion held together by a common thread of wonder, mystery, silence, and hope — a thread woven from an emerging vision erupting spontaneously from the depths of our psyches and the sacred heart of the universe.

The sacred impulse is an invitation to become spiders who create a pattern of relationships that is imaginatively responsive to the new cultural waves that are crashing on receptive shores of the twenty-first century.

The sacred impulse challenges us to develop networks of security and trust, new constellations of relationship that hold out the promise of profound integration as we soften the boundaries between intimacy and contemplation, feminine and masculine, action and reflection, and as we move forward with hope into a time of unprecedented harmony, balance, and peace.

ACTIVATING THE IMPULSE

The universe has labored for billions of years to reach a point in its complexification where it can now bring forth something through you.... What is needed now for the universe's unfolding story is not a new galaxy or a new star. What is needed now is a new form of human being. —BRIAN SWIMME

Life consistently presents us with challenges and change. One such challenge occurs when through a sacred impulse we begin to see the world differently and live out the implications of the new creation story through the following.

Childhood Memories. Through childhood memories we experience again the grandeur of creation, the beauty, power, mystery, and majesty of life.

We experience a deep mystical unity and know again the exaltation of existence.

~ We are rescued from a world of shopping malls and consumer relationships.

~ We experience again the flora and fauna of our childhood home — the rivers, strawberries, thunderstorms and boats, the many faces of creation.

The Creative Process. At its deepest level, creativity is living out the paschal event; we live and die to our mortality and rise to make a contribution that will live on after us.

~ The creative process confronts us with the forces of life, death, and rebirth.

~ At its heart the creative process is an impulse toward immortality — reaching for a way to give birth to a project, idea, or child that will live on after us.

Earth as Primary Sacrament. We are initiated into a vital relationship with the divine: the imagination erupts, the spirit stirs, the heart opens, and wisdom occurs in the recesses of our souls. Our path unfolds and we discover through self-expression intimacy with the divine, with humanity, and with the other-than-human world.

~ The natural work is our introduction into a living relationship with the divine through which we discover destiny, joy, and fulfillment.

A Listening Heart for the Poor. When we listen to the poor, the neglected child, the abused wife, the forsaken tree, or the polluted beach, our awareness expands and we feel closer to God. When we listen to the voiceless, our energy increases and we understand in new ways that the transformation of the planet is a spiritual task.

~ When we are receptive to the voice of the poor, we experience sacredness and are more present to what really matters.

Stories. Stories of ancestors and prophetic people alter our consciousness and inspire the spirit. Through stories we discover our origins in the context of our lives. In storytelling the passions of our heart become incarnate through form, figure, and word.

~ Stories name our relationships and make possible intimacy, love, and celebration. Stories invite forgiveness and dissolve projection, illusion, and false hope.

~ In storytelling we find our voice and discover our identity. Stories call us to justice, a justice that is tactile and passionate, igniting the flame of compassion and hope.

~ Stories are "shamans of the soul."

~ Through stories we know where we've been, where we are, and where we're going.

~ Stories of the universe and our own stories find their beginning in the heart of the universe.

~ Stories enhance our capacity to perceive how the patterns of our lives reveal a greater purpose.

~ Stories illuminate the moment.

~ Stories foster reciprocity and animate circles of wisdom and concern.

The Sacred Impulse. The Sacred Impulse is an inclination to act, a preoccupation that prompts us to respond — a nagging feeling, a hunch, an unplanned magnetic intuition, a movement from the inside out, an awareness of spirit that hovers over the cosmos and summons us to life.

~ The Sacred Impulse ignites the fire of our imaginations and the stirrings of the heart.

~ The Sacred Impulse is an eruption of the pulsating energy of God that calls us to love and compassion through the heart and fire of the cosmos and our lives.

~ The Sacred Impulse invites us to leave behind a worldview that is forced, static, and stuck.

~ We let go of a worldview that desacralizes life, denigrates the intellect, represses spontaneity, denies death, devalues story, memory, creativity, sacredness, the poor, and then blames the prophets and teachers of today.

~ The Sacred Impulse celebrates our epic of existence and summons us to insight and intimacy as we embrace more fully the heart and fire of our planetary journey.

The impulse that affirms is the impulse of the spirit that gives us breath and life.   —Ursula King

What follows are guidelines and structures for meetings — the integral process of a planetary spirituality: opportunities for friends and neighbors to gather and reflect on each of the chapters. It is my hope that through participating in these processes you will deepen your experience of community and discover new implications of a planetary spirituality.

Guidelines for Meetings

The Integral Process at the end of each chapter involves participation. These meetings are an important component of discovering the wisdom that resides within each member and finds expression in the gathered community or group. Each participant is encouraged to speak from the heart, to be fully present, and to listen to the contributions of others.

All participants will be invited to make their unique contributions, to share their stories in a context of trust and authenticity. The process will be punctuated by moments of gratitude, listening, silence, aesthetic responses, and actions. Responsibility for gathering and leading this circle will be rotated among the members. All members remain co-responsible for the guidelines themselves.

STRUCTURE OF THE MEETINGS

The process will begin with a welcome. Though the circle leader should be careful to avoid intrusive questions, the goal from the beginning is to engage in significant conversation.

Each of the chapters that follow will be the focus of reflection for two meetings. The initial gathering will be prepared for by reading the chapter in advance and preparing written responses to the questions posed at the end of the chapter. This process is in summary a reinvention of the "see, judge, and act" approach that was developed by Cardinal Joseph Cardijn in France and that was popular in the Catholic Action Movement of the Christian Family Movement, Young Christian Workers, and Young Christian Students. In the context of a planetary spirituality, however, "seeing" is to experience with compassion and mercy the impact of the world about us; "judging" is to decipher the causes and consequences of the oppression and woundedness that are perceived and experienced, whether political, cultural, economic, or ecological; and "acting" is to live out a planetary spirituality of creation and liberation, with our imaginations nourished and our spirits energized to bring about a new context for our lives. The Catholic Action process of see, judge, and act is also the foundation for base communities that are engaged in liberation theology in Latin America. The guidelines in these pages follow closely the articulation of this approach in the work of Brazilian theologian Leonardo Boff.

The second meeting devoted to each chapter will build on the first meeting. Each participant will bring an aesthetic response (for example, a poem, a piece of art, a picture, a musical recording). The meetings will generally begin with the lighting of a candle and a moment of silence.

After each participant has presented his or her "aesthetic response" to the group, the members will be invited to spend some time on their own (ten to twenty minutes) as they pay attention to what each member of the group has presented.

When the members reconvene, the conversation will be guided by the passing of a "talking stick." As the process continues, each respondent will have the full attention of the group members. As the talking stick is passed, each participant will retain the option of simply passing the stick on.

Questions or comments that the participants may wish to address regarding the aesthetic responses include: What do you see? Hear? Feel? What is your experience of the aesthetic response? What is your critical understanding? How do you feel prompted to act, based on your experience and reflection on the stimulus presented? Following each participant's personal response, a "significant conversation" will occur within the whole group. A theme or themes will be named as they are generated from the collective conversation.

A moment of silence follows, after which the group is invited to reflect together on the total experience of the gathering. The formal portion of the gathering concludes with a moment of meditation and gratitude.

As the program develops, groups will generally develop an experience of community. The members will learn to speak from their direct experience.

The Journey

Come with us on the journey
from stardust to wonder.
No need for baggage;
everything is within.

Wisdom is your compass,
curiosity your spark!
Release your presumptions;
step into the dark of the void.

It's a mystery, a sacred mystery.
Awaken to the universe.
Surrender to the story
that's unfolding for you and me!

— Sophia Center, Weekend Program

Chapter One

Our Vocational Destiny

*Vocation does not come from willfulness. It comes from listening.
... It means a calling that "I hear."* —Parker Palmer

One April I was in Washington, D.C., a city we tend to see through a lens created by the media. We think of the reports on crime, political duplicity, and military involvement around the globe — Desert Storm, Bosnia, Kosovo. But it is also the gathering place for hundreds of national organizations.

Furthermore, Washington is home to a tidal basin. There is an abundance of cherry blossoms in spring; countless monuments to past presidents, national heroes, and giants of science and industry; and a multitude of museums. The city houses a rich narrative of a nation's struggle, creativity, and human transcendence in the face of adversity.

The Franklin Delano Roosevelt Memorial tells the story of the president's courageous leadership and of a people who took up the challenge of economic depression and a world war. Roosevelt's profound belief in the human spirit has left us with a realizable impulse toward freedom. His words ring through the spirit of the country: "We have nothing to fear but fear itself."

The Holocaust Museum tells a story of terrible human suffering and terrifying human madness. It reminds us of one of the darkest moments in human history, the genocidal attacks on the Jewish people. This place demands that we remember. It reminds us of the undaunted resilience of the human spirit, so passionately crafted in the words of Elie Wiesel and others. We see images and diaries, some of which were buried in the Kovno Ghetto and later recovered as a sign of the resurgence of the spirit of the people who can now tell their story of tragedy and ultimate triumphant courage.

Washington is also the home of the Vietnam Memorial. The wall has row upon row of names of men and women who gave their lives or were missing in action in this unjust conflict. It has become a magnet for the pain of a people who on Veterans Day — and in fact every day — bring their tears along with gifts of flowers, cigarettes, and beer to this reminder of inhumanity and the misguided use of military power. Now, decades past, the Vietnam War remains a scar on the psyche of this country that can never be exorcised by punishing the poor and defenseless people of Iraq or other countries whose resources hold out the promise of a higher standard of life for the West.

Washington is also the home of the Albert Einstein Memorial, which recalls the joy and beauty of the universe. This welcoming sculpture reminds us of the unextinguished flame that burns brightly in the minds of a people, and of the enchanting and healing beauty that radiates from the heart of the universe itself.

In many ways, Washington is a microcosm of the universe's pain, beauty, birth, and memories. It is a context for aspirations, a place to explore the past. It reminds us of the undiminished flame that continues to burn brightly today, a flame nourished by the beauty of the natural world. Its entrancing presence is oxygen for the soul of a nation whose creativity and spiritual courage are remembered in the legacy of the past and the energizing focus of a hope-filled story yet to be told.

To fully comprehend and express the new worldview that is emerging into our psyches and our culture requires us to think symbolically; it is possible to grasp life's deepest mysteries only through metaphor, analogy, and myth.

Just as I walked around Washington on that April day, I invite you now to walk around your bioregion and hometown to discover the depth of your story and to look anew at your life and your vocation.

Each life is a chapter in the narrative of the universe that continues to unfold. As I peer into San Francisco Bay from my office on the campus of Holy Names College, years of history pass through my consciousness. At this moment, I feel a sense of past and present converging. The Golden Gate Bridge becomes a symbol of a link not only between past and present but also East and West. As my focus shifts from the capital to the Pacific Rim, I gain a new perspective.

I remember the layers of experiences that have laminated my life, significant moments from the past that bring forth a new realization of what it means to be here on these beautiful California shores. From my "window on the bay," I recall my journey from Canada, arriving in California to join an energetic movement that promised to transform the culture and reenergize the human spirit. As I gaze into San Francisco Bay, names flash before me, people who have come from cities like Dayton, Seattle, and Orlando, states like Oklahoma, Michigan, and North Carolina, and countries like Ireland, Australia, England, Guatemala, Canada, and Taiwan. Their lives and passions pulsate through my consciousness. They are people with dreams, wounds, and courageous questions who came here and then departed on journeys of joy, struggle, innovation, and accomplishment. They came with hopes and returned to transform their lives, their relationships, their lifestyles, and their work. As I reflect on the meaning of beauty, brokenness, and wisdom, I remember those who gathered here on their spiritual quest, listening to the voice of vocation.

THE CLASSROOM OF THE COSMOS

On a warm September afternoon I found myself thinking of the recent past. The pastel beauty of this final weekend of summer cloaked the Oakland hills and San Francisco Bay below. A group of us sat in a circle in the Heafey Building of Holy Names College and listened as we introduced ourselves. We announced who we were and where we lived and expressed our hopes and dreams for the program we were about to begin. We came with apprehensions and longings: preoccupations and questions about the mystery and meaning of our vocational destiny.

The bioregions from which we came had shaped the landscapes of our souls. Some arrived with heavy hearts from the bedsides of loved ones. Others were facing a crisis in a marriage or a crossroads in a career. We all wondered about the future. Despite our differences, we were all responding to the same palpable call, invited by the Earth and the cosmos in this critical time. We came to realize our purpose and participate in the great transition, to give expression to our historical mission, our place in the great work to which all humanity is called. We came to integrate our lives, fulfill our destiny, and become better able to inaugurate the new era that awaits us all.

We came with books, readers, and packets under our arms. We came with copies of the curriculum, yet somehow knowing that the primary text for our common journey resided in the recesses of our psyches and the revelatory moments of the universe itself. We came to take our place in a constellation of relationships with those we love and with others who will join us on the journey.

And we came to be architects of the new chapter in the unfolding story of the universe, the story that is told every morning by the sunrise, the soft dew on the grass, the breeze in the meadow, and the promise and mystery that become available to us as we peer through a telescope or a microscope.

We came to remember what we somehow genetically already knew and to express our gratitude for being children of the universe. We came in response to a mysterious call. We came to cultivate a listening heart. We came to remember our roots and to realize that our origins are signified by the stars and the stories that are told. We came to listen to the music of the universe — and to one another. We came on a spiritual quest. The words of Thomas Merton resonated for all of us as we tried to discover our reason for being here at this time:

> And if I never become what I am meant to be, but always remain what I am not, I shall spend eternity contradicting myself by being at once something and nothing, a life that wants to live and is dead, and a death that wants to be dead and cannot quite achieve its own death because it still has to exist.

The Call within the Call

Deep ecologist and Buddhist scholar Joanna Macy asserts that we live in a vocationless culture. Certainly, many people today, both young and old, are troubled and puzzled about their lives and the work they are called to do. Even though they have made choices earlier in life, they feel restless, unfulfilled. This crisis of vocation seems uniquely characteristic of our age and appears even among religious orders. In the Middle Ages, religious communities were formed whose members knew clearly what they were called to do.

Some started schools as educators; others opened hospitals. They built and staffed the institutions that became the infrastructure of medieval culture.

Today these same orders are divesting themselves of their institutions as their members search for other work to fulfill their personal and congregational purposes. Many people in the secular world deeply experience calls to generosity and service, yet realize that the so-called helping professions — teaching, law, medicine, and others — are no longer appropriate vehicles through which they can express their calling. Many of us, religious and laity alike, are still searching for the "call within the call."

I propose that, as new millennium people, we are being called to live in unprecedented ways. We are called to invent for ourselves and for those who will follow us the cultural implications of a new and living cosmology. Some of these implications will demand enormous change in our views of behavior and professions. Lawyers will be called to defend the rights of Earth and every species on it. Doctors will realize that they must support and foster the self-healing properties of the planet. Therapists will see themselves as companions who support the spiritual emergence of those who journey with them and whose lives are also an expression of an impulse toward health and wholeness. Theologians and ministers of religion will be called to focus their work more on creation than redemption. They will see themselves as reminders of the sacredness of life — and, in fact, of all existence. They will see their own lives and the narratives of their spiritual journeys as integral to the unfolding story of the universe itself.

If vocation is a call, what do I hear when I listen to the voice of vocation? The responses I receive in my listening are often puzzling and opaque even though at times some clarity emerges. The following propositions can help us find clarity in assessing the dimensions of the call.

An authentic call cannot be based on the abolition of the "true self." It cannot be based on conformity to the ideals and examples of others. Although we admire Martin Luther King, Jr., Mahatma Gandhi, Dorothy Day, Oscar Romero, and others, our true calling will not be discovered through imitating them or anyone else.

An authentic call is most often revealed in "moments of grace" when through unplanned events we experience our lives as deeply imbedded within the community of life, the dynamics of the seasons, the prompting of the spirit, and those unbidden insights that come to us through openings in the imagination.

An authentic call will become most available to us when we are willing to grope courageously with a listening heart into the mysterious terrain of divine presence.

An authentic call comes when we reflect on what most occupies our consciousness and invites us into the embrace of newfound freedom and self-transcendence.

An authentic call is "the DNA of the soul" wherein lie the seeds of destiny and purpose.

An authentic call resides within the fertile paradox of our cosmic journey that celebrates both the wonder of each revelatory moment and the adventurous foresight that invites us forward into a hopeful future.

Our response to the vocationless culture will require a magnificent effort, a new context, and a new calling. The result will be a new people and a new Earth. The path, though challenging, will be passionate and exciting. We will be called upon to confront difficult questions as we strive to build a new culture, one that can be a vehicle for transforming our lives and the entire Earth community.

Our call is fostered by a vision that celebrates our origins; a time when new energy becomes possible, awareness is activated, and we are inspired again.

Our call enriches our capacity to listen to what is emerging into consciousness and enables us to make choices that are in harmony with our inmost self.

Our call supports the impulse to explore the wisdom of our heart's deepest desire as the story of our life's unfolding becomes available to us.

Our call reminds us that the best things we have to offer in life are not yet named or understood, while we look toward the deeper meaning of our existence; we experience a greater intimacy with all that is.

Our call is revealed through relationships that are evoked and energized by moments of intimacy and profound paradox.

Through the primary sacrament of self-expression we discover the significance of our call and continually discover avenues of compassion that are waiting to be activated by our unique presence and zest for life.

WHAT I AM MEANT TO BE

Most of us can identify with these words of Thomas Merton; I know I can:

> I have no idea where I am going. I do not see the road ahead of me. I cannot know for certain where it will end. Nor do I really know myself.

I realize that what most deeply moves me and the longings that remain most profoundly in my heart are these: I want to know why I am here; and I want to belong to the people whom I serve and with whom I share a common journey. My heart aches when I fear that I have missed an opportunity to fulfill my purpose — whether in the context of a job opportunity, a location, a class, a relationship, a project, or a subtle movement of the spirit that I have let slip by without response. Throughout my life I have been confronted with the deep angst and longing to belong and to be available, to feel that I am and have been able to put my gifts as a person to the service of my community and planet.

This desire to fulfill my purpose—accompanied too often, unfortunately, by the conviction that I know best what I am to do with my life—brings to mind the old truism, "Man proposes, God disposes." Often I have felt deeply disappointed when my plan for my life has been "shattered," and I have found myself on a path that I would not have chosen. These new and unwanted roads always seem to involve more work, greater challenge, increased uncertainty, and an unknown outcome.

I have found that all that remains at times like these is the capacity to trust and keep moving, not to allow the shattering of dreams to suspend my efforts or diminish my desire to keep moving in the face of disappointment.

In many ways, these episodes in our lives seem to reflect our toxic culture, which also appears to have lost its way and given in to a proclivity toward death. We wonder why our country bombs other countries to preserve our own lifestyle, practices political duplicity that puts power before people, and values appearances before truth and authenticity. We lead dislocated lives in a disconnected society, part of a dysfunctional cosmology that allows pathology to reign.

Perhaps the most challenging spiritual exercise of this new millennium, this era of vocationless culture, will be the shift from illusion to reality. This is what Saul Alinsky, architect of community organization, was fond of calling the movement from the "world as we would like it to be" to the "world as it is."

This process is most challenging; it requires depth, determination, and willingness to embrace a life that is filled with neither fantasies nor regrets. While recognizing and accepting our past mistakes, we are called to nourish a deep-seated desire not to surrender to discouragement or despair. Rather, we can use disappointments of the past as fuel to reenergize our efforts and to achieve new goals. In some way, our individual lives, with all their demands and disappointments, enchantments and exaltations, are microcosms of the planetary challenge that confronts us: no less than creating the Earth anew. The outcome of this unprecedented, transformative moment is as yet unclear. We must, as Myles Horton says, "make the road by walking." Or, as Pierre Teilhard de Chardin put it, we must "go down into our inmost selves and there discover the wellsprings that we dare to call our lives."

Meeting the challenge will require an openness to a new kind of literacy, a language that will consist of perception, intuition, story, symbol, gesture, ritual, art, silence and sound, process and procession, stillness and movement. It will demand that we embrace ambiguity, live the question, enter the mystery, and experience a new humanity in a context that is functional, focused, and alive to the moment.

Discovering our vocational destiny is not a one-time effort, achievable in a semester class or a weekend workshop. It is an ongoing and lifelong process. It is, as a poster popular in the 1970s reminds us, "a journey, not a destination." Ultimately, of course, we are talking about experiencing the reality of love, an experience that animates our concern and affinity for the other, whether person, planet, or the divine. As we feel ourselves once again aligned with the deeper direction and consciousness of the cosmos itself, we will begin to comprehend the "call within the call" that has haunted us.

This new vision will involve a synthesis of the wisdom of science, mystical and prophetic traditions, women, indigenous peoples, and other groups that have not previously been heard. We will strive to create a culture that will foster new energy and a zest for life, a culture based on interaction and choice, identity and purpose, images and stories, values and structures that will give renewed expression to harmony, balance, and peace. This will be a culture that celebrates diversity and pluralism at every level — pluralism revealed in the lives and stories of people and groups whose diversity is manifest in language, lifestyle, temperament, economics, and a capacity for inclusion.

This new vision will be energized by a democratic approach to participation, decision-making, and problem-solving. The exciting result will be a balance between freedom and authority, function and structure, people and politics, humanity and Earth. This culture is in some ways already emerging whenever we are sensitive to and supportive of each person and each member of the living Earth community.

The vision being evoked and fostered in our time will be animated by increased levels of communication. The evolving relationships embodying this web of compassion and tapestry of life will be marked by touchstone categories of reciprocity, information, support, and common action. A sustaining vision will emerge from a prophetic group of people committed to their own transformation and the great work of cultural and planetary transition. The birth of this new culture into a truly ecological age will be fostered by a renewed sense of personal destiny, the practice of right livelihood, and the fulfillment that is realized through contributing to the historical mission to which all humanity is called.

This quest for our vocational destiny will require more than deep conviction. It will emerge out of a profound trust that our lives are in touch with the consciousness of the universe itself. Out of this dialogical process, we will discover the capacity to respond to the mysterious attractions that come to us from an intense desire to discover our place on the planet — our vocation and call.

REFLECTIONS

Threshold Moments. Sometimes the impact of living in a consumer culture devastates my spirit and erodes my soul. Questions demand answers, but those answers elude me. Where do dignity and destiny reside when every relationship is based on consumerism? Whether the envelope at church, the mortgage on the house, or the economic tie to a spouse, life seems reduced to money, power, and possession. Is it possible to avoid being reduced to an object — something meant only to be possessed, consumed, or destroyed? Is it possible to restore a sense of the intrinsic value of self, other, and the other-than-human world? There is so much domination and desecration in life, which seems harsh and problematic, bitter and burdensome. As I contemplate these questions, I long for a time now passed when life was simple and predictable, a time that I suspect exists only in my imagination.

Still, I remember with nostalgia my friends and classmates who graduated from high school and took positions in one of the nearby petrochemical plants. They had predictable employment. With secure jobs, they proceeded to marry, buy a home, raise a family, plan their retirement, and in general fulfill the life expectations of people who lived in the Great Lakes bioregion at the mouth of Lake Huron. Predictable. Secure. A way of life that seems lost in the emotional turmoil of modern choices and endless decision-making.

For many of us, life-changing events have occurred that we have only later come to understand as subtle moments of transformation. Perhaps the solution to what Joanna Macy called our "vocationless culture" is to be sensitive to moments of attraction or "allurement." In such moments, we feel drawn forth. Then, almost as an afterthought, we recognize that powerful transitions have taken place. We need to notice these moments and grasp their possibilities. Perhaps the issue is not the absence of vocation but awareness, not daring to follow the deeper promptings that we fear even to acknowledge.

Stories of Beginnings. We can think of beginnings as fodder for later resurrection moments — moments of grace, sacred impulses, and intuitions that emerge from the past. They show up in the present as expressions of unexpected possibilities. Beginnings are challenging, uplifting, and sometimes sad. They elevate the spirit while reminding us of what is lacking in our lives. These learning opportunities foster fresh energy and new life.

Celebrate the Fire. During the "winter blah" days — those days when a hunger for the sun fills our spirit — we are reminded of the importance of receptivity. We need to be grateful for the fire that heats our home, to allow others to warm our hearts, to be thankful for the sun's fire, which warms the Earth. We need to look into ourselves for the fire in our hearts and imaginations that ignites peace, hope, and creativity. We need to allow ourselves to warm and be warmed by that spirit that burns in and through us, the fire that will heal and bring spring to the winter of our "*spiritual* blahs." Celebrate the fire.

The World As It Is. As we have seen above, Saul Alinsky was fond of saying that "there's the world as it is and the world as we would like it to be." The way we work and our very lives change one into the other. Sometimes these changes are subtle — and sometimes they are misguided. The media may mislead us as they interpret reality through lenses of power or politics or economics. The media can condemn or idolize a public figure, start or stop a war, win or lose an election. The way we see life has a powerful effect on our efforts to change the world. But it also affects our day-to-day interactions. Our perceptions of people can allow their dignity to shine forth, or they can distort who they are. To invite ourselves to become who we are truly meant to be is a challenge and an opportunity.

The Meaning of Peace. Today we unfortunately have many opportunities to mourn the reality of war. But this sad reality leads us to reflect on a spirituality of interconnectedness that sees peace as the ultimate result of healing divisions and divisiveness. War becomes impossible when we see ourselves as one with the Earth and with each another; when boundaries collapse, peace is possible. When we pause to remember those who have died in the violence that is war, let us also celebrate our oneness, so that war will cease to be a category of our culture. In many ways, the Vietnam Memorial is a shrine of reconciliation, a place for forgiveness and an opportunity for healing.

The Meaning of Prayer. Prayer is being present to the beauty and the pain of life, finding language and symbols to express the inexpressible. Prayer is entering into those important moments in our own lives and the lives of others. Prayer may be contemplating a sunset. It may be reflecting on the issues of life: birth, love, work, wonder, and death. Prayer is interacting with and affirming the divine presence in all of life. Prayer is gratitude and acknowledgment. Prayer is the deepest desire of our life, through which the divine is revealed in our midst. Prayer is a conversation, sharing the burden, celebrating the excitement. Prayer is being with God in our journey through life.

Prayer means living in the soft embrace of divine energy that enfolds our presence and heals our pain. It is an opportunity to renew our deep-seated desire for a life of justice, peace, and renewed possibilities. Prayer is paying attention to the breath of life, to the reality of doubts, to what our world could be.

I believe in the exaltation of existence,
in the seamless garment that brings joy to our hearts.
I believe in our abundant planet
that emanates harmony from the fire of unexpected relatedness.
I believe in the radical rediscovery of a common cosmic calling
and in our sustaining story of heart, fire, and hope.

THE INTEGRAL PROCESS

Seeing

~ Describe your experience of beauty and enchantment that is evoked by your bioregion and nourishes your soul.

~ Bring and share examples of how the media manufactures a particular perception of the current crisis, including your experience of the vocational crisis.

~ What do you hear and see when you listen to the voice of vocation?

Judging

~ Reflect on the causes and consequences of the current state of the world and the absence of the experience of personal destiny.

~ Invite each person to compose a statement and draw an image of his or her experience of what is going on in today's culture.

~ As you reflect on your background, competencies, and contributions, what do you see as your place in humanity's historical mission?

Acting

~ As the members share their responses, have them place their compositions on the floor to form a mandala in the center of the room.

~ Include on the mandala a statement of your current understanding of your place in the "Great Work."

~ The group reports on actions planned before the next meeting.

Chapter Two

The New Story

I get energy from the Earth itself. I feel that as long as the Earth can make a spring every year, I can.... I won't give up until the Earth gives up.
—ALICE WALKER

It was a Thursday evening in October. From the college campus we could peer over the trees into the stately beauty of San Francisco, the city of Saint Francis. Its buildings loomed large and proud in the west. We had come to spend an evening with Thomas Berry.

The students presented an opening song entitled "The Faith of the Future," based on the writings of Pierre Teilhard de Chardin. Thomas Berry, in many ways a successor of Teilhard, is a cultural historian, cosmologist, and ecologist. He calls himself a "geologian." He is generally understood to be the most significant scholar and spokesman for the movement that sees the future of humanity and the entire planetary community as unfolding from a new cosmic story.

As the song ended and Berry took the microphone, the group in the crowded college chapel rose to its feet in spontaneous applause. We were expressing our gratitude for his presence among us and for his lifetime of dedication to making possible a more mutually enhancing relationship between humanity and the other-than-human world.

Berry reminded us of the beauty of the cosmos, the enchantment of the universe, and the challenge, danger, and possibilities
that await our children and all those yet to be born — of every
species. He stood there that evening as a voice for the voiceless, a
spokesman for the deep wisdom that resides in women, indigenous
people, our Christian roots, and the new science. With a twinkle in
his eye and a knowing smile, he reminded us of the need to nourish
our souls and amplify our spirits with the mystery of each meadow
and the gorgeous beauty of a sunset or a star.

Looking back over his more than eight decades of life, he called
forth from us a renewed awareness of our numinous destiny and
the legacy that is our rightful inheritance. He reminded us of the
danger of "soul death" during this "era of human pathos and ecological bereavement." He reminded us that if we devastate the
planet, we endanger and extinguish our souls, diminish our sensitivity, imagination, and depth, and lessen our capacity to taste,
see, feel, and hear. He challenged us to take back our souls and
the soul of our country, the soul of our planet. He warned us that
if we do not meet this challenge, we will exchange reverence for
utility, diversity for destruction, beauty for abuse, divinization for
degradation, our origins and stories for amnesia and autism, intimacy for alienation, restoration for ultimate damage, spontaneity
for despair, and healing for a culture of death.

He reminded us that out of the chaos and devastation of this moment can come an enormous creativity that could foster harmony
and integration for the entire Earth community. As he spoke of our
society's unique "moment of grace," a time of both chaos and promise, he reminded us that we have been chosen to live at this particular
time and that each of us has a unique and significant role to play
in our life. We have the opportunity to contribute to the transition
from the postindustrial era to the ecological age that awaits us. This
new age can be an era of celebration, of enjoyment, of savoring ex-

istence and experiencing entrancement as we gaze at the flow of a river, the twinkle of a star, the beauty of a tree, and all that engages us in intimacy, relationship, and reciprocity. The new era can nourish us and engage our capacities for play, delight, and good work. Berry promised us that if we undertake this Great Work, we will know where we are, where we have been, and where we are going.

Life in the new cosmology becomes a paradox, a context that is both serene and dangerous, a community of life where human children can survive only if the children of every species also survive. Each species is called — as we are called — to contribute to the overall health and integrity of the planet. We are called to build a society that reveres the New Story, that communicates to us how the Earth functions and how the divine is present in everyday life. In this New Story, the *principle of differentiation* honors and asserts the differences that are ever-present in the universe, while *interiority* names the inner spontaneity and personality of every species, and *communion* bonds everything, acknowledging its relationship to everything else.

At this moment in history, we are experiencing a period of transformation when we are called to commune with the universe, to experience the beauty and extravagance of the cosmos. We are to fashion a life that reflects that New Story, that story of the universe, which is in fact the only seamless garment there is.

Author and poet Alice Walker tells a story that is germane here. When she was a young girl, she was noted in her family and community as a beautiful child — vivacious, playful, buoyant, and admired by all who knew her.

One day, while she was playing in the backyard with her brothers, one of them shot her in the eye with the BB gun he had gotten for Christmas. Alice was immediately blinded in that eye and had a noticeable scar afterwards. As she grew up, this accident, this blight on her beauty, became a source of great pain, embarrassment, and

shame. Years later, when she herself became a mother, she often
wondered what her daughter thought about her eye. She was afraid
that somehow this mark would diminish her in her daughter's eyes.
Then one evening, when she was leaning over the bed as her daughter was going to sleep, the little girl gazed up at her mother and said,
"Mama, you've got the world in your eye."

The little girl had been watching her favorite television show
that day, "The Big Blue Planet." When she looked into the blue-
white scar in her mother's eye, she was reminded of that blue jewel,
the Earth. When Alice Walker gazed at herself in the mirror that
evening, she felt the pain, shame, and embarrassment of the years
melt away. The words of innocence and wonder spoken by her
daughter had brought about a healing. This moment expanded
into a fresh appreciation of herself, the wonder of her life, and the
beauty of the planet itself.

Although our experiences are different from those of Alice
Walker, each of us has also experienced beauty and brokenness in
many aspects of our lives. We are like the shattered chalice on the
sanctuary floor in Leonard Bernstein's Mass — each particle emanating light and beauty from its place and state of brokenness.
When we surrender our addiction to the lifestyles and worldviews
that contribute to a culture of death and domination, to industrial
rubble and planetary devastation, we experience the same emotions that Alice Walker experienced when she saw her scar through
the eyes of her child.

Like the human body, Earth is subject to disease. Its circula-
tory system, its rivers and transportation routes, are blocked —
like the Bay Bridge between Oakland and San Francisco in rush
hour. Its cities and factories are spread like a cancer over green
space, with the population growing exponentially, doubling every
forty years and out of control. Fertilizers, toxic sprays, and acid rain
undermine and weaken its immune system.

Recently I was on Prince Edward Island. After a rain, I gazed into a pond and saw hundreds of dead fish poisoned by the runoff from the potato fields. We need to confront the human pathos and ecological bereavement that encompass our culture and cloud our perspective. We need to develop the capacity to see and foster beauty, to awaken to the depths of devastation and heal it.

Like Alice Walker before the mirror or an astronaut gazing back at Earth from outer space, we as a people stand poised on the precipice of new beginnings and new insights into our beauty, balance, and brokenness. To negotiate the transition we are facing will require nothing less than a shattering of old categories, worldviews, and perceptions of our broken planet. Only then can we grasp new insights and comprehend the beauty that surrounds us — partaking in the cosmic unfolding that Berry and others call the New Story. Only as we surrender our "old" story of shame, limitation, and woundedness can we embrace this New Story, in which brokenness becomes beauty and a listening heart.

This seamless garment, this interconnected tapestry, this woven web of life is the New Story of the universe. This New Story is breaking through into human consciousness. It is sacred and revelatory, even though it is not written down in canonical texts like the Bible or the Koran. Rather, the New Story is told through the great epic of evolution, those great transformational events that have occurred over time and that include the emerging role of humanity today. This New Story provides us with the opportunity to ruminate on life's greatest questions, including what the historical mission of humanity is at this critical moment in the unfolding life of the planet.

The New Story resides in the mystical and prophetic consciousness of those who desire and seek a deeper experience of the divine through the world's great wisdom traditions. And the New Story finds expression in our own lives, each one of us a paragraph of intensity and adventure whose unitive consciousness embraces the beauty and goodness of creation. In the lives of mystics, both medieval and modern — Hildegarde of Bingen, Francis of Assisi, Meister Eckhart, Thomas Merton, Pierre Teilhard de Chardin, and others — there is an awareness that the energy of the divine is profoundly present throughout all creation. The mystics invite us to activate our imagination while exploring the deeper mysteries of birth, death, human reinvention, culture, and creation itself.

The New Story is also told by the shamans and indigenous people of the world, all those whose cosmology is holistic and integrative of body and spirit. The Story springs forth from all that heals dualisms, that understands justice as geo-justice (personal, social, *and* ecological), that fosters engagement in life rather than passive withdrawal, that promotes interconnectedness between women and men, nature and cosmos, humanity and Earth.

The New Story is also being revealed to us through the wisdom of gender. The feminine archetype of inclusion and interconnectedness transforms domination into participation. This ontological feminine principle challenges and transforms hierarchical dualism and the structures that oppress and inhibit the full development of humanity, both men and women, as well as the other-than-human world.

Yet another wisdom source, the wisdom of science, returns us to our common origins. The science of the New Story is not a science of materialism. Rather, it is deeply mystical and sacramental, seeing creation as a psychic-spiritual reality and evolution as rooted and centered in the divine, whose presence is in all things. Such a view of science invites and fosters a dynamic involvement in our physical, human, and other-than-human world.

The New Story is revealed to us moment by moment in images and sounds: sunlight and darkness, the song of the birds and the rustle of the breeze, the flow of the river and the dizzying heights of a mountaintop, the stateliness of a tree, the cry of a coyote. The

Story gives voice to the universe, a chorus that invites us to become vital participants in the universe itself.

The New Story...

Speaks to us of the divine in all things.

Reveals the dynamic principles that are operative in all of life — difference, depth, and interconnectedness.

Dissolves separateness, fosters interiority, and creates community.

Reminds us of our embodiment and our embeddedness in the dynamics of Earth and all that is.

Calls us as humans to a role of co-responsibility and reciprocity with our planet. If we are successful, we will have clean air, pure water, wholesome food, healthy children, shelter for everyone, planetary peace, respect among nations, and a sustainable future.

As we ponder life's significant questions, at this time of transformation and new beginnings, the New Story can sustain us as we create a viable culture to give meaning to our existence. The New Story can empower us to undergo an archetypal exodus and move forward with new confidence and grace!

As we reflect on and tell this New Story, we return to the memories of our childhood, and we recall our hopes and sacred impulses to respect and celebrate the intrinsic value, dignity, and freedom of every species. In these moments — these epiphanies — of hope, challenge, and possibility, we look back and listen, and then we move forward to new decisions and actions. We become "hospice workers" for dying institutions and a dying cosmology and "midwives" for a new culture and the New Story being born and told in

our midst. Together we create a "web of life" that joins all our stories: stories of mystery and enchantment; paschal mystery stories
of pleasure and pain, genesis and cosmic crucifixion, beauty and
devastation, intimacy and alienation, Easter and Pentecost; stories
that remind us that we are even *more* than our stories, that we can
support and enrich one another on our continuing journey.

Will we heed the prophets like St. Francis, Saul Alinsky, Hildegarde of Bingen, Pierre Teilhard de Chardin, Paulo Freire, and
others on whose shoulders we stand and whose calls from the past
echo in our day?

The New Story touches each of us in a unique way. It has been
told in my life through those moments when creation touched my
soul and I realized that every place is home.

REFLECTIONS

Every Place Is Home: A Story of Place. Sometimes I feel over-
whelmed. I seem to know so little about the important things.
When I study the origins of the universe and reflect upon my place
in it, my mind seems stretched beyond its capacity and incapable
of embracing the full meaning of this great mystery. Only a frag-
ment seems available through my comprehension. In the face of
this mystery, which is both elusive and engaging, I am suddenly
flooded with recollections that remind me of the sacredness of life.
I am touched by the cosmos when I recall:

> Lying in bed late at night in the summertime, listening to the
> frogs chirp vigorously in the pond outside my window near
> the railway tracks.

> Drinking with great gusto the sweet liquid that drained in
> the springtime from the generous trunk of the maple tree
> that stood so strong and stately beyond my kitchen door.

Fearing the torrential rain that accompanied the tornado sweeping through my neighborhood, lifting rooftops and trees as my family and I stood transfixed at the awesome power that had just been unleashed among us.

Taking in the enchanting sight of a rainbow that arched through the sky, showering me with its beauty as the sunlight broke through the clouds when the storm had ceased.

Sitting on the porch with my father in our village home on a summer evening, enjoying the cool breeze that drifted in off the river.

Listening to the familiar sounds of the foghorns and train whistles that echoed from the boats on the St. Clair and the freight trains on the tracks behind the house.

Drinking in the stillness and silence that accompanied the winter's first snow or the welcome melody of a mourning dove at dawn.

Laughing in joyful surprise at the eruption of a pickerel from the silky surface of the St. Clair at sunset.

Breathing in the new life of spring, when the crocuses burst forth, the snow melted, and the sun brought warmth to the frozen soil.

Basking in the heat of summer, with the growth of the grain, the lightning, thunder, heat, and welcome rain, and the baseball games that for me presaged the game of life.

Changing pace in the fall, with the gold, red, yellow, and orange of the autumn leaves, the bronze of the wheat field, the crisp air, the bounty of harvest.

Appreciating the rigor and cold of winter, the invitation of the frigid air to ponder the possibilities of life and the promise of a fresh existence, to discover the beauty of ice floes on the river, the snow enveloping the fields, the sparrows searching for food on Earth's white carpet, and the blackbirds devouring with zest and vigor the bread crumbs and suet and seeds we provided for them in bird feeders in the backyard.

Half-dreaming in the nights when the moon hung full and golden in the sky, illuminating the night and bathing my bedroom with the penetrating light that shone through the darkness.

All these were expressions of my bioregion, with its trees, waterways, land, and sky — my place on the planet, my cosmic home, a classroom and a sanctuary, a catechism and a church, an extended family and a history lesson, a story with chapters of wonder, beauty, struggle, gratitude, and God.

My place on the planet has taught me that every place is home, every place is sacred, every place is support for maturity, a context for awakening, a locus for belonging, an interdependence, a book of revelatory moments that communicate the sacredness of life.

The Story and Our Call. An integration within the human community is taking place through the unfolding of our common story. Listening anew to the ancient insights of indigenous people, we expand our vision of what the human journey is. Through watching and listening, we begin to grasp more fully what the universe is truly like. We begin to see our lives as chapters of the story of Earth. Through knowing this story, our story, Earth's story, we can more fully appreciate water, soil, and each species. As we recognize our origins, we see more clearly where we are and what we must do. From the emerging energies of our new ways of seeing and of remembering, we fashion a new community with one another and with Earth.

The Language of Life. Today we are challenged to see our faith through the eyes of the discoveries of the new science, the contributions of artists and mystics, and the experience of ultimate reality that is rooted in our tradition. There is without doubt a dynamic interrelationship between ourselves and the rest of the universe. The primary language of our new understanding is storytelling. We are learning that storytelling radicalizes us, grounds us in our own existence, and enables us to navigate the waters of life. Stories are revelatory and liberating. Take time today to tell and to listen. It is important.

In
the dark
of the moon,
in flying snow,
in the dead of winter,
war spreading,
families dying,
the world in danger,
I
walk
the
rocky
hillsides
sowing
clover.

— WENDELL BERRY

THE INTEGRAL PROCESS

We live in a time when fear, hope, and freedom are in every heart and every lip; a time when more and more people are embarking on a spiritual journey marked by openness and risk — a journey that is deep, energetic, creative, and compassionate...inspired by the New Story.

The young people today are torn by disconnection and despair. In their search for beauty, they discover that their lives are intruded upon by war, ecological devastation, the misuse of drugs, and the insatiable seductiveness of advertising that pushes them into conformity. How are we called to pass the torch to the young of today who are the adults of tomorrow?

> It is the experience of touching the pain of others that is the key to change. It is not the book or the class or the idea that changes us. As important as these things are, it is the experience. Invariably it is the experience of crossing over boundaries, touching someone else's reality, and hearing others' stories that changes people.   —JIM WALLIS

Seeing

~ What indicators of cultural pathology are you aware of in your home, neighborhood, workplace, bioregion?

~ What response comes to you from these questions?

~ How has the consumer society become the religion of the day?

~ How can we evoke and experience hope, especially among the youth in a society that espouses a culture of death? How does the New Story and a living cosmology provide a basis for hope, fresh energy, and a zest for life?

~ In what way can a spirituality that fosters a fascination for the beauty of creation, combined with the praxis approach of liberation theology, contribute to the healing required at this moment of grace in our culture?

Judging

~ How can a renewed appreciation for the beauty of the cosmos and the challenges presented to us in our day awaken us to a new sensitivity, imagination, and depth?

~ In what way can a sense of the sacred in all life evoke a transformative response from each of us?

~ How do your friendships in this circle of friends foster new ways of appreciating existence and the epiphanies that come to us each moment?

~ Explore how your experiences of school, work, and church challenge or legitimize the cultural pathology that intrudes upon our souls and permeates the dynamics of our institutions and existence.

~ Describe how the New Story gives hope to your life and provides fresh understandings for your tradition to empower you to confront the separation and domination that permeates our society.

Acting

~ Spend some time reflecting on the New Story as introduced in this chapter. Consider how you might introduce the New Story.

~ Is there any way you might interact with young people, and in fact people of all ages, to hear their stories and offer your perspective on how each story is a chapter in this New Story?

This New Story of the universe and our place within it is meant to renew the spiritual insights and practices lying at the core of our tradition.

The new cosmology may help us to renew and relive the spiritual wonder and wisdom that our tradition once embodied, and from which we have become so alienated.

The new scientific cosmology shows us a universe in which we have an origin, an inclusive home, and a meaningful destiny.

— PAUL BROCKELMAN

Chapter Three

A Dynamic Relationship

*Rising like a Phoenix from the ashes is a justice that is sweet
but not timid; that heals rather than continues to divide; that
has the creative energy of the cosmos behind it rather than the
temporary death engine of our own outrage, pain, and fear. A
justice that returns honor to all the beings involved. A justice that
is juicy, life affirming, creative and glorious. I think the worlds of
suffering and the ideas of justice are healed and brought to a state
of wholeness only in the heart of each one of us. From there our
voices can join in a song that cannot be ignored.* —ROBERT GRAY

Gathered in a comfortable meeting room in an education center adjacent to the campus of the Catholic University of America
in Washington, D.C., a group had come in response to an invitation to explore what might emerge from a dialogue among
people engaged in social justice, spirituality, and church reform.
They came to share their doubts, reflect on their fears, celebrate
what most energizes them, and name what they see as the frontiers
of their work. They came to weave the contours of new relationships and deepen the tapestry of connections already made.
The room became bright with electricity and new ideas. In this
small center in the nation's capital, names and mailing lists became

transformed into people and conversations. The group members found their perspectives challenged and their ideas examined. This gathering of people from different places and different areas of work proclaimed a commitment to alleviate poverty wherever it exists and to extend their preferential option to the poor and to poor Earth.

They rededicated their lives to the discovery of meaning and the healing of suffering and injustice. They examined the questions and commitments that placed them in solidarity with those on the underside of life. They explored the ideas, values, relationships, structures, and practices that shaped their perspective and animated their energies for renewal, justice, and depth. They came to name their spiritual journey, to see their spirituality and life as action, to discover the poem that resides in each of their souls, and to renew their appreciation of goodness, beauty, brokenness, and love. They redeclared their commitment to inclusivity, openness, and peace. They came to honor an integral spirituality that can refresh and energize their lives. They pledged their determination to develop a listening heart, especially to the voiceless and most abused of every species.

One way of responding to this time is to see ourselves as hospice workers for a culture that needs to die with dignity, a culture whose primary forms of education, religion, politics, and economics need to be radically changed. Our call is also to be animators of new cultural forms that will align society to the New Story, a holistic educational project, an economics that considers the "gross Earth product" rather than the gross national product, a political system that advocates and supports the rights of all species, and a theology that fosters the beauty and blessing that is present in all of life. Just as shoots of grass find their way through the concrete in our cities, so the new genesis of culture and hope will break through in our consciousness and in our lives — if we let it.

A Spiritual Awakening

One response to this critical yet hopeful moment is a reawakened interest in spirituality. This often leads to a growing ambivalence in our attitude toward institutions, which may express itself in an increased trust in our own experience. (On the other hand, we can respond by becoming more dependent, even codependent, on fundamentalist and conservative institutions. There is ample evidence that both options are being taken today.)

The prophets of our time have provided us with wonderful images and language for this breakthrough moment in our human journey. Teilhard de Chardin, for example, writes, "I went down into my inmost self, and there I found the wellspring that I dare to call my life." Liberation theologian Gustavo Gutiérrez tells us that "we drink from our own wells." Joanna Macy wrote of "the great turning." For for all of us, spirituality is about deeply imbibing the waters of life, about savoring, embracing, and quenching our thirst through an experience of the divine.

Spirituality is certainly unique to each of us, based on our individual experience, but it is also possible to name characteristics of a planetary spirituality that are common to all of us. These include:

Our spiritual narrative — the unfolding of our own story with Earth in mind.

Reverence and a sense of the sacred. We revere creation for its own sake, not only for its usefulness. For example, we celebrate the tree for its beauty rather than seeing it only as a resource for lumber or paper.

Appreciation of the wisdom of the senses. The experience of the divine happens through our senses. Thus creation becomes a primary sacrament and source of mystical union with the divine.

Membership in the community of life, a sense of responsibility for ourselves, others, and all creation.

Commitment to tradition and continuity with the past combined with innovation and assimilation of new viewpoints.

Such a spirituality can:

Satisfy our hunger for the divine.

Bring us joy, vitality, playfulness, fresh psychic energy, and a zest for life.

Catalyze transformation and help us realize our potential.

Release the sacred impulse in our lives.

Nourish our psyche, feed our soul, and liberate our body.

Stimulate a "metaphysics of goodness" as we expand our capacity to savor beauty and experience enchantment.

Amplify our sensitivities through opening our heart and providing new perspectives on hopes, dreams, struggles, and accomplishments.

Evoke in us a profound experience of gratitude for being born at this particular "cosmological moment."

Invite us to a new spiritual practice whereby we "think cosmologically and act globally and locally," a spiritual practice that encourages us to increasingly accept, foster, and protect the entire Earth community.

Awaken us to an "incarnational consciousness" — that is, lead us to recognize those places where the divine intersects with the human in our lives. (To make this rather abstract concept

concrete, reflect on these questions: Where is Bethlehem today? What new is being born in our culture, on our planet,
and in the recesses of our hearts and minds?)

Acknowledge justice-making as a genetic act, a moment of
newness, an act of love, a work of the heart that extends into
and embraces our psyche, society, and Earth.

Provide an organic continuity between the natural world and
human social forms.

A planetary spirituality will take up the challenges to cherish, amplify, and protect our zest for life and the psychic energy necessary
to respond to the problems and possibilities of our time.

GALAXIES AND THE RECESSES OF THE SOUL

The spiritual quest reveals at its heart a profound paradox. As
Thomas Merton said, "We have what we seek. We don't have to
run after it; it was there all the time, and if we give it time, it will
make itself known to us." He also warned us, "If I never become
who I'm supposed to be, I will spend the rest of my life contradict-
ing myself." A great comfort in our search was provided by spiritual
writer Henri Nouwen, who reminded us that we are called to be
wounded healers, "to recognize the sufferings of our time in our
own heart and make that recognition the starting point of service,
to enter into a dislocated world... [that] will not be perceived as
authentic unless it comes from a heart wounded by the suffering
about which it speaks." Our spiritual journey is as much an embracing of "en*dark*enment" as en*light*enment. It is a journey into
silence, a context in which to face our fears, to embrace the cosmic
shadow as well our own shadow, to discover a home for our pain,
and to realize that our pain is a teacher. Our goal is not to escape

life but to embrace it, to find a home for it in our journey, and to allow it to be our teacher.

Our spiritual journey and the quest of our lives can be regarded as a movement from narcissism to mysticism, a journey from inordinate self-consciousness to a liberating embrace of all that is, a celebration and savoring of an unmediated experience with the divine, which evokes ecstasy and awe.

Along the way, we come to a realization of the limits of our existence, a deep knowing that we are both divine and also not God. We move toward a willingness to relinquish the presuppositions that we bring to our lives, and we engage in an "ego death" that can cleanse us of illusion and false consciousness. We see that each of us is called to a particular place on the planet, that each of us is uniquely gifted and uniquely summoned to fulfill the purpose and destiny of our existence.

Our spiritual quest will be realized and fostered through the practice of listening, a capacity to respond to inner promptings, to engage in dialogue with all expressions of the community of life, and to embrace courageously the mystery that continues to present itself in the form of unanswered questions. In other words, never put a period where the divine has put a question mark. Or, as the poet Rainer Maria Rilke wrote, "Be patient with all that is unsolved in your heart. Try to love the questions themselves, like locked rooms, and like books that are written in a foreign tongue.... Live the questions."

The spiritual quest will always require and be revealed in relationship and dialogue.

A Dynamic Integration

Rosemary Radford Ruether tells of a lecture she gave after the release of her book *Gaia and God*. The room was crowded as people gathered to hear her perceptions of the Earth as a living and conscious being. But later in her talk, when she began to connect the Gaia hypothesis with the call to justice, several people left the room.

Ruether's story illustrates the challenge that we face today to create a dynamic integration of the New Story of the universe and the story of geo-justice as it presents itself in the cry of the poor and the cry of Earth. When we reflect together on the state of contemporary culture, we can affirm the words of the philosopher Martin Heidigger, who described our present context as being enveloped in "tranquilized obviousness." In other words, our conscience and our consciousness are affected by a "cultural trance" that diminishes our critical awareness, reduces our sensitivity to pathos and devastation, and robs us of the sacred impulse to respond. Social ethicist Joe Holland describes our present situation in these words: "We are right now in the midst of one of the most traumatic, yet creative, cultural transformations of all human history . . . , a cultural earthquake." And cosmologist, ecologist, and cultural historian Thomas Berry names this time in human history a "moment of grace," a time of profound transformation, unprecedented challenge, peril, and possibility.

The question that presents itself is this: How do we experience and express an integration between the spirituality that flows out of the New Story and a commitment to justice? Posed another way: How is geo-justice the natural and dynamic outcome and application of the New Story of the universe? Many of us have a variety of experiences with even the term *justice* and its implication for our lives. Too often the language of justice itself evokes our "religious feelings" and becomes a system of ethical norms, shoulds, and musts—a guilt-driven sense of obligation.

But justice is, in fact, about healing. It evokes in us, when properly understood and connected to the New Story, a new consciousness, new symbols, new culture, and a new spirituality, an *engaged* spirituality. Justice requires a capacity for and celebration of relationships: relationships between our intrapsychic experiences and our social systems, a deep connection between our interior life and the outer aspects or systems and structures involved in transformation. Properly understood, justice evokes the biblical mandate to "heal what is broken and renew the face of the Earth," to create a new heaven and a new Earth. A justice that flows from the New Story will provide us with a fresh sense of equity among self, others, and creation. A renewed view of justice will foster in each of us a deep intention to carry out the historical mission to which we are called, to participate in the great transitions taking place in our time, to restore creation to its pristine beauty, and to restructure society to a greater degree of mutuality and magnificence.

This new vision of justice, which flows from a new cosmology, will energize an intimate balance between consciousness and conscience, mysticism and prophecy, the new story and the dynamics inherent in the universe. The outcome, hopefully, will be personal, social, and ecological harmony, balance, and peace. The new justice will provide a perspective and an approach that will enhance critical reflection and be healing and transformative. We will learn again to listen to the *anawim* — the voiceless, the little ones of God. Through listening, we will "grow our soul," experience the sacred, and become animators of prophetic responses, actions that flow from the energy and unitive embrace of a mystical consciousness, responses that find expression in a loyal disobedience by which we become architects for a "prescription for rebellion" rather than surrendering to the seductiveness of a "culture of conformity." A renewed vision of justice will flow from the formation and experience of base communities and support groups of mutual interdependence, which will foster alternative approaches of relationship and hope. Justice — geo-justice — as it flows from the new cosmic story will be itself an expression of the deepest dimension of every person. Justice will be a spiritual practice, a practice that fosters a response of concern and care for self, others, and the entire Earth community. This expression of justice will find its source in the wisdom that resides within the recesses of each of us and within all aspects of creation.

How can justice become integral and essential to our spirituality? How can it challenge our conventional understandings of prayer, meditation, and retreat from the world? How can justice permeate our lives and propel us to engage the world? How can justice be a vehicle of listening and recognition? How does justice result from a balance between nature and society? How can justice lead us to risk and to participate in timely action? How is justice at its core radical and revolutionary (a catalyst for change)? How does justice engage us in the paschal practice whereby we "die to ourselves" and "rise to a concern for the other"? How is justice ultimately about cosmic order and love?

As Muriel Rukeyser wrote, "The universe is made up of stories, not atoms." So, we ask ourselves, How does the New Story shape our understanding of culture? Perhaps some of the following are indicators of this new and developing understanding and relationship:

A holistic psychology that embraces not only the psyche but also the systems within which we live and interact.

A democratized political system that offers full participation, both in the ballot box and in our neighborhoods, so that people can express their own voice, as well as give voice to others.

An ethics that validates the intrinsic value of all things, that celebrates, honors, and protects the rain forest, the mammals, the ozone layer, and the human child.

A society that acknowledges and honors human culture in its many and diverse forms — color, tradition, history, art, and practice.

The New Story, when we properly understand and practice it, will energize our commitment to a sustainable community of life, one in which we meet the needs of the entire Earth community without endangering the resources and life systems for future generations.

Geo-Justice: A Preferential Option for Earth

"Social injustice has an ecological face," wrote Elizabeth Johnson. "The aim is to establish and protect healthy ecosystems where all living creatures can flourish." Diarmuid O'Murchu stated, "Today we use terms like *geo-justice* to describe the essential connection between the personal and the ecological, the spiritual and the earthly, aspects of our call to be justice-makers." And Leonard Boff wrote: "We are co-piloting the current phase of the evolutionary process in tandem with the guiding principles of the universe."

The work of geo-justice starts as an act of self-discovery. Meister Eckhart said, "If you want to discover who you are, do justice." Geo-justice is also the foundation and basis for authentic relationships. Again, Meister Eckhart guides us when he wrote, "If you understand what I have to say about justice, you will understand everything I have to say." Based on this process of self-discovery and right relationship, we are challenged to develop an *analogical imagination*. This basically means taking what we have learned in our new cosmology and applying it on the personal and social levels.

The three principles that are operative in the universe — differentiation, interiority, and communion — can provide the framework for geo-justice. For example, differentiation looks at the local level, in all its creativity and uniqueness; interiority functions at the depth of human experience, which we call psychosocial; and communion is the global component that calls us to compassion for all creation. Geo-justice becomes the process of remembering the New Story and living out its implications in our lives. Remembering, rather than learning or discovering, reminds us of our common origin with the universe itself, for we are all made from stardust. We have within our genetic coding the cellular memory that we now call the New Story. When that New Story becomes conscious and we find analogies and applications for it in our contemporary culture, we will have achieved the goal of geo-justice and activated what many would call the analogical imagination.

Ecological justice can go hand in hand with personal and social justice. Leonardo Boff reminds us that schoolchildren need more than classrooms; they also need pure water and sanitation to be able to learn. Geo-justice is a response to and a language for this interrelationship. Geo-justice brings together a passion for brokenness and for beauty. Geo-justice dynamically integrates the story of the universe and the story of personal, social, and ecological justice. Geo-justice provides us with a new form of awareness and self-realization. Geo-justice reminds us that we are located in the universe and connected to a vast constellation of existence, a constellation of relationships that are both singular and unique. Geo-justice reminds us that we are called to see ourselves as members of the family of life as well as the human family.

We can look at geo-justice as presenting us with the challenge of creating a *transgenetic coding*. For example, ants are genetically coded for community and in every case will express that coding through an anthill. As humans, we are genetically coded for compassion; however, the symbols, language, structures, and images of that compassion are ours to create. The particularities

are not predetermined. Geo-justice, then, becomes our transla-
tion of the New Story into cultural form. As Elizabeth Johnson
writes, "Contemporary science is discovering a natural world that
is surprisingly dynamic, organic, self-organizing, indeterminate,
chancy, and open to the unknown." And therefore geo-justice
continues to pose the questions: What is the implication of the
New Story in cultural form? How do we create a vehicle that is
responsive to the fear, grief, and anonymity of the human and
other-than-human world? How do we put into practice a vision
of inclusion, radical interdependence, and intercommunion? How
do we practice geo-justice and foster a respect for the otherness of
all beings, supporting their right to exist and at the same time taking action to remove the societal structures that oppress both their
freedom and their lives?

I propose that geo-justice will result in a culture that is organic, differentiated, feminine, communitarian, and always open
to change. Geo-justice understood in this way will support those
aspects of creation that are spontaneous, cosmic, and connected,
and that promote an understanding of humanity whereby we see
ourselves as related to the whole of life. Geo-justice will presume
that everything that the human sees, does, and thinks will be ac-
complished with Earth in mind. Geo-justice, then, on its deepest
level, will be more about being than doing, a listening spirituality that sees Earth and every species as a source of story and
divine communication. It is a planetary spirituality of engagement
and application that joins the universe and a personal, social, and
ecological culture.

Geo-justice is when differentiation celebrates difference, interiority celebrates depth, and communion becomes an indication of
compassion. Not only are these principles present in cultural form,
but we see through them a glimpse of the divine — differentiation
as the source of the Creator, interiority as the sign of the Word,

and communion as the indication of the Spirit. We then begin to understand that when geo-justice happens, we have a trinitarian culture, and the divine becomes present in our midst. In the words of Thomas Berry, "Geo-justice can be a way to guide and inspire our lives."

Margaret Wheatley, in her important book *Leadership and the New Science,* wrote: "Improvisation is the saving skill. We play a crucial role in selecting the melody, setting the tempo, establishing the way and inviting the players — when it works we sit back amazed and grateful." In a way, we could say that the practice of geo-justice is an improvisational practice. It is the work of the cultural artist.

There can be no rigid blueprint of implementation. Many authors and cultural workers in the past have been reluctant to articulate a methodology, for fear that it would be rigidly practiced and rob the practitioner of the spontaneity and creativity that are needed in each particular context and cultural moment. Thomas Moore underlined this important perspective when he wrote, "I won't give any concrete suggestions of what to do. My conviction is that deep changes in life happen through movements in the imagination." Geo-justice is such an act of creativity, spontaneity, and improvisation and needs to be left open to the breath of the Spirit.

Fritjof Capra highlighted this perspective when he wrote, "Only if we perceive the world differently will we be able to act differently. So we need a change of perception, a shift in paradigms in our thinking and in our values. We need a shift from fragmentation to wholeness, from a mechanistic view of the world to an ecological view, from domination to partnership, from quantity to quality, from expansion to conversation, from efficiency to sustainability." So geo-justice, then, is evolutionary, organic, improvisational, spontaneous, and unfolding. It's about living the question rather than fixating on predetermined results. It's about

entering into mystery, about responding to a magnetic intuition
that invites us into a prolonged engagement with life. Geo-justice
challenges us to be vulnerable and open to a "photosynthesis of the
soul" — a moment of sacredness and possibility when we become
fully present to life, to its mystery, to its patterns, its vulnerabili-
ties, and its strengths. It's more about imagination and less about
a predetermined path.

As we reflect on the questions of justice and the role of geo-
justice in the practice of our new cosmology, many questions
arise. The following may serve as a springboard to pondering the
connection between the New Story and geo-justice:

- What do you feel about justice?

- What was your first and/or most memorable act of justice-
  making?

- Who most exemplifies justice-making for you?

- How do you understand geo-justice?

- What questions do you have about geo-justice?

- Is listening the first act of geo-justice?

Components of Geo-Justice

Geo-justice happens when the principles of the universe — differentiation, interiority, and communion — find expression in
cultural form. At that moment, geo-justice becomes a response
to a personal and planetary challenge to discover the converging
terrain between personal, social, and ecological justice, a passionate and practical call and response through action that opens us to
the beauty and brokenness of our time. Geo-justice is a new way
of seeing and acting cosmologically. Geo-justice, then, becomes a

context for the rebirth of images, stories, myths — all of life — from within, below, and outside existing cultural forms.

Geo-justice touches our lives and our planet on many levels. For example, the livelihood of a person in a Third World country may depend on cutting down the trees of a rain forest. That is the *local level*. But through the eyes of geo-justice, that local endeavor for economic survival, for food and shelter, becomes a planetary issue as well: it confronts us with an ecological peril that is planetary in scope. That is the *global level*. We become ecologically vulnerable when we rob Earth of its trees, our source of oxygen, the "lungs of the Earth." The destruction of the rain forest has profound personal and psychological implications for all. That is the *psychosocial level*.

Global-Communion-Spirit. The first component of geo-justice is the global component. It flows from our awareness of the principle of communion in the universe: the realization that everything is related and interconnected, that we are cousin and kin to the entire Earth community. Brother David Steindl-Rast wrote, "Mystical awareness is the deepest anchor for global solidarity." This experience enables us to feel united to Earth as a whole and simultaneously discover ourselves upon it. The global component expresses an experience of community that brings us awe, wonder, and beauty. We discover through the global component of geo-justice, and the unitive consciousness that accompanies it, common images for our common work. This global component supports our approach to interdependence as we become architects of a transcultural planet. Through the global component, we experience ourselves as residents of the "global village." Justice flows from this awareness as we experience a deep communion with all that is and with the planet itself. We become enveloped in this spirit of transformation that permeates all of life.

Local-Differentiation-Creator. The second component of geo-justice flows from the principle of differentiation and finds its cultural expression in the language of the local component; this is the place from which the story flows.

The local component supports and fosters prophetic and imaginative actions in the concrete context of our lives. In the words of Paulo Freire, we become "wet with the soul of the people." And Thomas Berry wrote: "In an acceptable cultural context, we would recognize that the unique properties of each reality determine its value both for the individual and for the community. These are fulfilled in each other. Violation of the individual is an assault on the community." At the local level, our ecological, social, and personal concerns are reflected in awareness — for example, knowledge of the fact that toxic dump sites are built in minority neighborhoods. At the local level, we take up the challenge of our bioregion, those specific waterways, hills, trees, and flowers that make up our home on the planet. This local context, our bioregional home, this particular place on the planet, is where we are called to live out our story and weave it into the tapestry of the universe and geo-justice. The local component of geo-justice becomes a place to listen, to recognize, and to support those significant ones who see victory in the struggle and hope in the capacity to work for the rights of all members of the Earth community. Properly understood, the local component of geo-justice can be practiced in a fourfold way.

First is the *moment of hope,* when people are invited to share their dreams, their stories, and the possibilities that they would like to see realized in their local situation. This is the *preorganizing phase.*

Second, other people in the neighborhood and bioregion must be invited to let go of the oppressive structures that rob them of their freedom, that hold them back, and that perpetrate injustice. This is the *disorganizing phase,* and many people find it both threatening and frightening.

Third, the people involved, all those who will eventually give birth to the new structures and forms that will support the local Earth community, must work together to name their problems and find solutions. This is the *organizing phase.*

Fourth, the culmination of this process comes when these new forms of justice-making join with the preexisting ones to bring about the change and transformations to which all of the people of the local community are called. This is the *reorganizing phase.* Our geo-justice work at the local level will be guided by the principles of nonviolence with an abiding respect for property, person, and principle.

Psycho-Social-Interiority-Word. The third component of geo-justice involves the dynamic relationship between personal experience and the larger society. Stan Grof, a psychiatrist and researcher in human consciousness, wrote, "The human psyche is essentially commensurate with the whole universe and all of existence." Thomas Berry pointed out that "our psychology is Earth-derived." And Paulo Freire spoke of "a common striving toward awareness of reality and toward self-awareness." In the words of these perceptive cultural workers, we see outlined the significance of the psychosocial component of geo-justice. It involves a dynamic balance between the psyche and society. In this component, the psyche is linked to and seen as a microcosm of society as a whole. In this dynamic, every aspect of our life becomes an instrument of planetary peace. The psychosocial approach sees personal (psychological) processes as instruments of expressions of social dynamics and change.

One way of describing the relationship between the psychological and the social is to look at it through the lens of social analysis

and psychoanalysis. In psychoanalysis, we are confronted with issues in our lives and predicate them on the lack of resolution of
our emotional issues. In other words, if something goes wrong,
whether systemic or emotional, the tendency is to blame ourselves.

Alternatively, social analysis tends to find the roots of problems
in the structures of society. Its tendency is to predicate the problem on oppressive systems. In my view, both of these approaches
are inadequate. It is impossible, I believe, to be an agent of struc-
tural change unless we have a deep personal self-awareness that
some of our energy for change has its source in our unresolved
personal problems. Unless we acknowledge that, we will tend to
lack a real sensitivity to the systems and fail to understand how to
change them.

In fact, we could simply be engaged in projection instead of cor-
rection of an unjust structure. It's possible that we are shouting at
the mayor because something is wrong in our neighborhood —
and it is also possible that this civic leader is really taking the brunt
of our rage toward a parent or some other shadow from our past.
It is equally true that if we run into resistance and difficulties,
whether from structures or our own unresolved emotions, there
is a predetermined tendency in society to say that the problems
exist because our psyche and emotions are as yet unresolved, that if
we could resolve the personal and psychological difficulties of our
lives, then peace would happen and justice would reign. Unfortunately, such an attitude is a trap. We need to engage in personal
healing and systemic change in a dialectical way that acknowledges
that the question is never one or the other, the psychological or the
social, but both together.

An important approach to consciousness research that has been
fostered in the work of Ken Wilber and Stan Grof is described as
spectrum psychology. In this approach, the psyche is viewed in four
different ways.

The first is *sensory awakening,* which describes the total body experience through the movement of energy, breath, and awareness. It has its foundation in the work and writings of Wilhelm Reich.

The second dimension of the psyche is the *biographical.* This focuses on memories and repressed material, both in the psyche and in the body itself, and finds its approach in both the recollection and reliving of these memories to free us from internalized and embodied traumas. This approach is based on the work of Sigmund Freud.

The third aspect of the psyche is commonly understood as the *perinatal,* that is, those events that took place before, during, and after our birth. The original psychoanalytic tradition understood the human as coming into life as a *tabula rasa,* a blank tablet. Otto Rank departed from Freud and his colleagues when he posited that the human psyche was profoundly affected by the events before, during, and after birth. This understanding has a great deal to do with our comprehension of the creative process and the analogies between human birth and the births that take place in the imagination.

The fourth dimension of spectrum psychology is commonly understood today as the *transpersonal.* Some call it an interface between psychology and spirituality, or sacred spirituality, where there is a departure from the confines of time and space. Perhaps the psyche identifies with some creature or, at a deep mystical level, transcends the confines of the reality described in the Cartesian/Newtonian paradigm. One of the most significant practitioners of this approach was Carl Jung.

The resolution of the psychosocial component will promote ecological concerns, consideration for humanity, and an increased compassion for all of life.

SHARED BEGINNINGS

The New Story reminds us of our common origins. We are "cousins" to each other in the sacred universe with a spirituality that can be described as an awakening to the depths, the unfolding of our story with Earth in mind. From this narrative approach, justice-making becomes an experience of equity and healing, a source of energy for dealing with resistance and oppression as we move toward liberation. Geo-justice expresses the human task at this time of profound transition and accelerated change. It challenges us to create a dynamic integration between the story of the universe and the story of justice.

Ralph Waldo Emerson asserted that "he who has not visited the house of pain has but seen half the universe." Pain is not only fuel for our journey, but it also a vehicle by which we enhance our humanity and become whole and healed and achieve our full personhood. This is the reality in our personal lives, but I suggest that it is also true in the larger context of the struggle for justice and the efforts to achieve liberation from oppression. Pain is again the vehicle by which we become more human, by which society becomes more just, and by which our planet can become more whole and healthy again.

Ecofeminism makes the connection between the pain and oppression of women and the devastation of the planet. In a similar way, geo-justice reminds us that in the work of racial equality, gender balance, and class equality, there is also pain, but out of this pain can come the social and ecological justice that is both a challenge and an opportunity for a healthy planet. In some mysterious way, geo-justice and the effort to bring it about become the vehicle to liberate the environmental refugees of our time, those who live in our cities, and every species, including the young and those yet to be born.

Recently, the city of Detroit witnessed a benchmark in its evolution. When I was a child, it was a great adventure to visit the J. L. Hudson Company, a large department store on Woodward Avenue. This great landmark — in some way the heart of the post-industrial flourishing of America's Motor City — was leveled to the ground. It was an ending, an acknowledgment that its customers had fled the cities to the suburbs, that the automobile industry had finally reaped its reward: urban blight and environmental toxicity. It also was a moment, said the mayor of Detroit, for new beginnings, for a renaissance in one of America's most historic urban areas. Yet, it still symbolizes all that confronts us now, all our grief for what has happened to the bioregions of our youth and the urban areas of our adult years, for all that has happened to our families and friends, for the health threats from cancer, AIDS, heart disease, and chronic fatigue syndrome, which have become the illnesses of our time.

Perhaps the deep lesson here is that we cannot bypass the Earth or avoid the pain of the planet, whether it manifests itself in toxic dump sites, the abuse of children, or the slow decay of our urban centers.

Things can change. I recall the five-year-old child from a minority neighborhood who had tears in his eyes at the end of an afternoon visit to a local park. When asked why he was crying, he sobbed, "Do we have to leave the park?" Only later did we learn that this was the first time in his five years of existence that he had had the chance to play in the park. The afternoon had been a significant moment of liberation for him, a spiritual moment, and he was saddened at the prospect of returning to the asphalt-and-concrete neighborhood where he lived. Perhaps his experience, both his tears and his joy, can be a metaphor for beauty and brokenness and an energizing focus for the work of geo-justice. The joyful/sorrowful child reminds us that justice is both personal and planetary; it is about both celebration and grief; it must be mediated by the beauty and the brokenness both of Earth and of all our lives.

REFLECTIONS

Search for Self. There is a "stormy search for the self" happening in many of our lives: emotional upheaval abounds, spiritual crises explode. Global crises constantly occur. Tragedy, doubt, and annihilation overshadow every concern. Within this framework, we journey — pilgrims on this planet, people whose pain, when properly understood and responded to, provides opportunities for expanding and deepening our spiritual journey. All of life is within the envelope of faith and spirituality. In fact, it is in these moments of insecurity and uncertainty that we are most often reminded of God's action in our lives. These moments are invitations to a more profound awareness of divine action in our lives.

Dualism. The Western world is dualistic. We tend to divide everything into two categories: we/they, black/white, male/female, being/acting, Earth/humankind, and so on. We often fail to see the connectedness between our inmost being and the cosmos, a connection that is at one and the same time enveloped in the divine. We need to understand that the divisions are not "out there" but in our language and in our minds.

Phases of Relationship. Every relationship has three phases: the honeymoon, the working through, and the resolution. Working through means taking the insights of our lives, the breakthroughs, and going into them more and more deeply until they become coded into the very pattern of our being. This process of deepening our understanding is the way we resolve life's questions.

And with each resolution, we enter into the quest for our deeper purpose. The process is a dance between ambiguity and clarity, between commitment and open-endedness, between intimacy and contemplation.

Healing and Wholeness. Healing is closely aligned with beauty. To restore our psyche and soul from the effects of exhaustion, stress, and pain, we would do well to enter consciously into the splendor of the physical world. A walk through the fields, a hike to the mountains, a swim in the lake, a deep breath of sea air are salutary for the soul. The harmony, compassion, and balance of nature bring their healing properties to our exhausted spirits. Nature can be our healer, our therapist, our companion, and our exemplar of inner peace.

A Litany for Transformation

Trust needs to be born,
Security needs to die;
Liberation needs to be born,
Oppression needs to die;
Celebration needs to be born,
Boredom needs to die;
Connectedness needs to be born,
Alienation needs to die;
Global awareness needs to be born,
Nation-state-ism needs to die;
Creativity and courage need to be born,
Fear of death needs to die;
The right brain needs to be born,
The left brain needs to be happy about it;

Feminism needs to be born,
Patriarchy needs to die;
Soul-making needs to be born,
Individualism needs to die;
Recovery needs to be born,
Addiction needs to die;
Playing together needs to be born,
Competing needs to die;
The Ecological Age needs to be born,
Environmental genocide needs to die;
Reverence for all life needs to be born,
Domination and objectification need to die;
Doing-with needs to be born,
Doing-for needs to die;
Be-attitude needs to be born,
Have-attitude needs to die;
Hope needs to be born,
Despair needs to die;
Creative silence needs to be born,
Empty noise needs to die;
Awareness needs to be born,
Insensitivity needs to die;
Circles need to be born,
Hierarchies need to die;
Dialectic needs to be born,
Dualism needs to die;
Laughter and tears need to be born,
Sadness and sentimentality need to die;
A new order of geo-justice needs to be born,
The old order needs to die.

THE INTEGRAL PROCESS

The injustices so palpable and present in our day impinge upon our psyches and capture our available energy. This leaves us immobilized and frozen by ecological disasters and wars of dominance that punctuate our global landscape, leaving many mystified and passive.

What can a people, energized by the new cosmology, say to a planet in pain? That pain is reflected in the faces of children, farmers, displaced persons in our inner cities, social and environmental refugees, and endangered species. The "lunar-like landscape" is the aftermath of clear-cutting, fertilization, pesticides, schoolyard assassinations, culture wars, aggression against women, genocide against indigenous peoples, and religiously motivated conflicts that burn senselessly in many parts of the planet.

Seeing

~ Take an inventory of the occasions and acts of injustice that you are aware of in your bioregion, in the institutions with which you interact (church, corporations, government).

~ What do you feel, think, and respond to from your collective awareness of injustice?

~ What does the new cosmology have to tell us about justice-making?

~ How can we fashion a new and dynamic integration between the story of the universe and the story of personal, social, and ecological justice (geo-justice)?

~ How can we work to create cultural expressions of the three principles of the universe: differentiation, interiority, and communion?

Judging

~ As you survey the injustices that are present to your awareness, reflect on the causes and consequences of these injustices.

~ How does your understanding of the new cosmology and your awareness of geo-justice assist you in comprehending the magnitude of the problems and the concerns that confront us?

~ Looking at the world through the window of geo-justice, how would you imagine an Earth community of harmony, balance, and peace?

~ How would you visualize the integration between the New Story and the work of geo-justice that will result in a healthy and hope-filled world?

Acting

~ Consider what concrete action you and your group might undertake to begin to heal the injustice that is present in the human-Earth community.

Life is an adventure of passion, risk, danger, laughter, beauty, love, a burning curiosity to go with the action, to see what it's all about, to reach for a pattern of meaning, to burn one's bridges because you're never going to go back anyway and to live to the end.

—SAUL ALINSKY

Chapter Four

The Spiritual Journey

Spirituality deals with the bedrock of human existence — why we are here, where we are going, and how we can comport ourselves with dignity along the way — struggling against oneself and against one's times.
— PHILIP ZAKESKI

CELEBRATING EARTH

It was Holy Week at the Springbank Renewal Center, a retreat center nestled in the rural countryside of Kingstree, South Carolina. The Holy Thursday meal had been celebrated, a simple yet profound memorial of the Last Supper. Plans were under way for the ceremonies for Good Friday. Central to the planning session was Karla, a wise and creative Franciscan sister, who for more than a decade had dedicated herself to honoring the wisdom in Native American spirituality. The focus of our Good Friday ritual would be the Native American sweat-lodge ceremony.

Early Friday afternoon, under Karla's gentle guidance, we began by preparing the sacred fire. After lighting it, we carried rocks and wood to the fire pit. We marked the four directions and gave thanks for the gifts we had received from Earth and all creation. At 3:00 p.m., the traditional time when Christians around the world remember the death of Jesus, we entered the sweat lodge and one by one proclaimed our connection to the entire Earth community, using the Native American mantra "All My Relations."

As we huddled in a circle, the flap of the sweat lodge was closed by the fire keepers, and we were enveloped in total darkness. Hot rocks had been brought to the lodge by the fire keepers and placed in the center of the circle. Karla poured water over the rocks. The steam emanating from the rocks represented the tears of Mother Earth and the cleansing that each of us longs for from the toxins of our own lives. As Karla poured the water, chants filled the lodge. Then she invited each of us to offer our prayers — in silence or aloud — for self, other, children, peers, and the planet itself. The final ceremony expressed our gratitude and compassion for all that is and all that will be.

Throughout this ancient spiritual ceremony, I remembered the Good Fridays of my earlier years. I recalled that, in our village in Canada, Good Friday always seemed to bring rain. Our parents would bring us into the house about noon to say the rosary. And then we would go to church for what seemed to be endless hours.

But there was something turbulent about Good Friday. It seemed to me that at 3:00 o'clock on Good Friday afternoon, the universe itself was stirring, almost groaning at the moment of Jesus' death.

And here, on the plains of South Carolina, the sweat lodge seemed an appropriate place on Good Friday for a restless heart, a place to recall powerful memories about death, ambiguity, and longings for new life.

That afternoon, I felt that the sweat lodge had become a womb, a cauldron bubbling with new life, a container that embraced the stirrings in my soul, a vehicle through which resurrection could become a palpable and powerful experience.

The time between that afternoon and the following evening was a period of quiet meditation. On Saturday night, we returned to the fire pit outside the lodge. With the flap open, the rocks cooled, and no one inside, it had become an empty tomb. We lit the fire from the ashes that remained from Good Friday in order to dispel the darkness, to realize again that the empty tomb is a deep reminder of the resurrection and an affirmation of a sacred impulse toward new life.

A woman lit the paschal candle from the fire and then lit her own candle from that. I blessed the new fire, lit my candle from it, and passed the fire to the candle of the person next to me. The fire was then passed around the circle, one by one.

Then, in silent procession, we returned to the retreat center, where we participated in the Cosmic Walk, a ritual that begins with the origin of the universe approximately thirteen billion years ago and unfolds through the galactic period, the Earth period, the period of life on Earth, to the relatively new moment of humanity on Earth.

Together we made our Easter by walking this evolutionary journey, celebrating the story that we are. We named our salvation history by hearing the words of Genesis and Exodus before we marked the birth of Jesus and heard the resurrection story in Luke. Then each of us walked to the center of the spiral in the middle of the room and retrieved two stones from a basket by the paschal candle. These stones represented the bones of our ancestors, our story, and our connection to Earth. As we returned from the center of the room, one by one, we clicked our stones together. When everyone had returned from the center of the spiral, we formed a circle and proclaimed our names. When it was my turn, I shouted out, "The universe resurrects Jim!"

Two participants, Lois and Joanne, then moved the paschal candle, representing the original fireball and the new life of Easter, to a table that held a basin of water. The fire reminded us that we share a common story that begins with the universe itself. The water represented the power to give life but also the capacity for death. As we "renewed our baptism," Lois and Joanne sprinkled us with water to remind us of the moisture of springtime and the liquid possibilities of newness everywhere. We then sang together the alleluias of Easter, formed a circle of solidarity, and recited together a eucharistic prayer of thanksgiving as we shared the simple and ancient meal of bread and wine. With our ceremony complete, we proclaimed in song the new life that we had just celebrated and that was so evident in the springtime beauty of South Carolina, a reminder of sacredness and fresh energy that would endure in our hearts and minds in the days ahead.

The tomb awakened us to both emptiness and new life, somehow engendering hope and expectation while dimming the terror of death and reconciling us to it. With newfound courage, we embraced each moment, confident of a glorious future, as we remembered with wonder the moments of our past. With flowers, bonnets, bunnies, and eggs, we paraded on life's stage and celebrated new possibilities as we made our Easter with Earth.

Crisis and Healing. As we talked over brunch on that Easter morning, we reflected on the context of our lives. Being at the beginning and the end of something is extremely exciting. It's like watching a trapeze artist at work: the flyer lets go of the bar and reaches out, expecting the catcher to be there. Most of us are like that flyer. We've let go of our old paradigm with the expectation that the new one will be there for us.

We are experiencing a cultural earthquake. We know from our own experience that something unsettling is happening. Yet life does not seem to be working quite right; there is an energy that wants to move through us, but it can't. I call that "psychic congestion." When the colon gets stopped up, nothing flows. Now the creative energy of the universe wants to move through us as we become who we are meant to be. When we put up obstacles to this flow, internally or otherwise, a crisis shows up in our life. That crisis could be a divorce. It could be the loss of a job. It could be a health problem. It could be looking in the mirror in the morning and saying, "Who is this person? What am I going to do with my life? Does life have a deeper meaning? Is there something that I'm missing?" Such crises, I believe, are personal aftershocks of the cultural earthquake. We are searching for who we are, for our place in the great work, our purpose and destiny.

A man once told me that he loved crisis. "I know if there is a crisis in my life," he said, "that I'm getting back on the track. A boil builds and breaks, and then something heals." Our lives are like that. I'm not saying that we *need* crisis, because if we are true to ourselves, then we can avoid it. But most of us, at one time or another, have these moments of crossroads and confusion.

Finding Our Place. How do we find our personal place on the planet? One of the ways, I believe, is to know where we are wounded. My childhood was disrupted by my mother's illness. As an adult in therapy, I realized that I was trying to heal myself by healing others who had similar wounds. I believe that if we research our pain, we will find where our avenues of energy are. It is not the only way, but it is one way. Henri Nouwen advised us "to recognize the sufferings of the times in our own heart and make that recognition the starting point of service; to enter into a dislocated world. Relating to a compulsive generation will not be perceived as authentic unless it comes from the heart — wounded by the same suffering about which it speaks."

Another way of talking about place is through the metaphor of homecoming. People often say, "I feel at home," or "It's like coming home." Home is the place where everything begins. Wendell Berry, Kentucky farmer and poet, wrote, "The world can't be discovered by a journey of miles, no matter how long. Only by a spiritual journey — a journey very arduous and humble and joyful by which we arrive at the ground at our feet, where we learn to be at home."

Our spiritual journey has already begun. To know that we are not alone in this journey is important. And we need to keep moving, because we can get "stuck" in pleasure — or in pain, which many have more practice in. We can also get stuck in creativity, which most of us would probably like to do. Ironically, we can even get stuck in justice, which becomes a "how to" and an "ought to" rather than a joyful undertaking. As we move through pleasure and pain and creativity and compassion in an expanding process of change, we can help each other by being soulmates, fellow travelers, on the journey.

Dag Hammarskjöld wrote, "I don't know who or what put the question. I don't even know when it was put. I don't even remember answering. But at some moment I did answer 'yes' to someone or something. And from that hour I was certain that existence was meaningful, and therefore my life was self-surrendered and whole."

A Planetary Journey. Something is dying, something new is being born, and we are in between. We are moving from a redemption-centered theology to a creation theology. The same is true in another cultural context: education. When we walk into a classroom, a predictable reaction from our past is that we do not know anything, that the teacher has all the knowledge. That is redemption-centered thinking in the classroom. But Paulo Freire writes, "What is education anyway? Education is knowing that you know. Not being told. It's knowing that you know." We reflect on our understandings in such a way that we are conscious of what we understand. We *all* contribute to the process. That is really empowering. That's building the strength and rigor of a spirituality that offers strength for our time in history. The truth is that none of us has the answers. We each have our own questions.

When we walk into a doctor's office, we are perceived as parts and as pathological. That is redemption-centered thinking in medicine. Contrast that with holistic medicine, a wellness approach, in which the organism is helped to heal itself. If we apply this to any discipline, we see how this kind of thinking permeates the culture. Whether we call it ignorance, or illness, or sin, it is everywhere.

We cannot animate people with despair. We must start with hope. So a planetary spirituality starts with pleasure and beauty and befriending. Meister Eckhart said, "When I was born, all creation stood up and shouted, 'There is God!'" Not a bad way to start.

Creation, blessing, celebration, enjoyment. The medieval English mystic Julian of Norwich invented the word *enjoy*. She wrote, "True thanking is to *enjoy* God." Our experience of pleasure is healing and a source of change. St. Thomas Aquinas claimed that pleasure changes us more than anything else. The question we should ask ourselves on our spiritual journey is, "How much pleasure are we having in our lives — how much deep joy?" As the new paradigm emerges, for which the planetary spirituality is an energizing force, we move toward a new cosmic consciousness, a celebration of the body and sexuality.

We must see the divine in *everything*. Meister Eckhart said, "Every creature is a word about God." God's revelation did not stop with the death of the last apostle; it is continually unfolding in our midst. Meister Eckhart pointed out, "If I could spend enough time with a caterpillar, I would never have to prepare another sermon.... Is-ness is God. This little caterpillar contains everything; microcosm, macrocosm, the entire universe is in that caterpillar."

THE REDEMPTION QUESTION

During an eco-spirituality class at the Graduate Theological Union in Berkeley, the conversation ranged widely on many questions. Of particular interest that day was the place of redemption in our Christian tradition.

Understood as Jesus' compassionate response to humanity's fallen state, redemption is commonly held to be the "saving act" by the Son of God because we as a people had "missed the mark." A prior condition for this apology on our behalf is an acceptance of the notion of "original sin." Although commonly accepted, "original sin" has never been clearly defused.

From a planetary spirituality perspective we can say that the current awareness of "original sin" is itself evolving. Understood in this way, original sin can be described as our resistance to mortality and to seeing death as a transition to new life, an incapacity to embrace the paradox of the incarnation: the realization that we are divine and at the same time finite. Leonardo Boff writes that we are "spirit open to the infinite but condemned to live in the finite.... To refuse to accept death in oneself as a necessary transition toward life beyond this life...this is what original sin means in human beings."

In planetary spirituality "redemption" reveals a restoration of relatedness, a transcendence from a narcissism and an inordinate self-consciousness that prompts humanity to render creation for its own use; new willingness to see grace, gratitude, and connectedness fully experienced and expressed in our lives. Properly understood redemption reminds us of a legacy of original grace, not just for humanity, but for all creation — all of us together enveloped in the compassionate embrace of the divine, each hopeful and encouraged by the anticipation of new forms of beauty, ongoing and co-created.

As the class came to a close that evening at GTU, though the question was not fully resolved, I knew we had explored a key question that is central to the Christian tradition.

Celebrating Art

J. Robert Oppenheimer wrote, "There are children playing in the street who could solve some of my top problems in physics, because they have modes of sensory perception that I lost long ago."

Recently, I was sitting in the airport outside Denver. The man sitting next to me said that he was a scientist, and that his work was exploring the meaning of vacuums. I thought that was interesting because we used to think of a vacuum as simply empty space. But with quantum theory — and quantum theology — we can say with confidence that a vacuum is a place in which creativity happens, where newness is born.

Today we are challenged to be creative. History tells us that disequilibrium is a precondition for change and transformation, both personally and culturally. Philosophers, historians, and scientists are introducing us into a process-oriented world, a new context for living, a new context for embodiment, for wilderness, for transformation of self and society. We can anticipate new stories, new myths, and the reinvention of our traditions, our psyches, and our political practices. We will recognize new archetypes — new ways of life, in fact — a new humanity, a new species whose task will be to re-create the face of Earth. Such a task will move us beyond the personal process to global awareness.

This new awareness, interestingly enough, will be enhanced by the practice of an old art — silence. In silence we learn to connect more deeply to our inmost self, to our sacred impulses, and to distinguish our inner process from the demands and emotional swirls that surround us. When we peel back the distractions that are so prevalent, we will be able, perhaps for the first time, to give birth to our true authentic self. This process of the soul will be deepened by meditation, by bodywork, by attention, by movement from illusion to reality, and by moments of "sabbatical time," when we can focus on the creative process and liberate our imaginations. "When imagination is allowed to move to deep places," said Thomas Moore, "the sacred is revealed."

George Cabot Lodge observed, "We are in the midst of a great transformation, comparable to the one that confronted medievalism and shook its institutions to the ground. The old ideas and assumptions that made our institutions legitimate are being eroded." It is, then, no surprise that creativity has not been welcome in bureaucratic and patriarchal structures. It is a neglected category in most spiritual traditions. Creativity is far too unpredictable — a force that has its own intrinsic logic and direction. Nobody can be told how to be creative. As J. Robert Oppenheimer noted, children are naturally creative. By the time they are about ten, however, this creativity has usually been squeezed out of them.

A therapist friend of mine in Toronto was doing a group process many years ago. The group consisted of students and colleagues. At the end of the session, one of the therapist's colleagues said, "Lea, why are you such a creative therapist? What are your credentials?" Lea replied, "In my life, I've experienced great joy and I've felt real pain. Those are my credentials." I think this expresses the dynamic of creation theology. Creativity flows out of pleasure and pain. All of us want to be more creative. Teilhard de Chardin talked about *cosmogenesis* — even the universe is continually creating. And theologian Gregory Baum reminds us that "faith resides in the imagination more than in the intellect." What people believe in is what they create.

Meister Eckhart's image of creativity is riding a horse. Trust the horse that's in you. You ride a horse and say, "My God, this thing's going to throw me off! I'm not sure where it's going." That's creativity. Trust the horse. Trust the desire. Trust the pain. Trust the anger. Trust the outrage. Trust the savoring. Trust the sacred impulse.

Meister Eckhart also said that creativity is "that which flows out and remains within." Think about that. For example, as a parent you give children life, you give them love, you give them up. Unless we let go of our images, they will never become whole.

In the development of the universe, sexuality and death came into existence at the same time. When we give birth to our images, we die — at least a little — in the process. Writing a book, preparing a sermon, having a conversation, making love, birthing a child — all these are acts of creativity. When I was trained as a community organizer, the basic question was, "What are you angry at?" The question has changed since then. Now it is, "What do you want to create?" Certainly, there is anger in creativity, but creativity is a much deeper process. Education is also a creative process: it is about creating knowledge. Creativity is disturbing and turbulent; nothing remains the same when we create. The process resembles the experience of sailing. In the beginning, as the boat leaves the shore, the waters are calm. As the process proceeds, we find ourselves out at sea, on turbulent waters. Similarly, the imagination erupts in the act of creativity, and unexpected energy tosses us to and fro on these unsettling, yet fascinating waters.

The creative process is a powerful reminder of our mortality. In fact, it is the way we strive for *im*mortality. As the child, the poem, the book, the painting, or the project lives on after us, we reach for resurrection and somehow transcend our mortality. Popcorn provides an apt if humble image for the process: something about to burst free in unpredictable ways.

We cannot create everything. Pleasure and pain are about being; creativity and compassion are about doing. Every opportunity that presents itself to us will never recur: jobs, relationships, even impulses to random acts of kindness. The creative process forces us to make a choice and go with it. And creativity is not always rewarded. When Ernest Becker had a book party on the publication of *The Denial of Death,* only six people showed up. After his death, the book became a Pulitzer Prize winner. Many acts of creativity are *never* recognized.

Anyone who has taken piano lessons knows that playing the piano takes effort and discipline. To play well requires commitment. But, like any art form, piano playing can also be a healing practice, a way to embrace moments of surprise or grief or celebration. Thomas Moore recalls that when he was informed of the assassination of Martin Luther King, Jr., he went to the piano and played for hours.

At the heart of creativity is an appreciation of difference. The universe teaches us that each expression of creation, each member of the Earth community, carries within it the unique presence and manifestation of the divine. St. Thomas Aquinas speculated that the divine could not reproduce itself in any *one* act of creation, and thus we have this multiplicity of beauty, of species, of members of the Earth community. So we not only honor diversity, but we claim our own uniqueness, our own gifts, as expressions of the divine. When we are tempted to think of God as distant and unchanging, the creative process reminds us that the divine is *always* creating, *always* in the act of change. We are called to participate in this same process. Creativity at this time of accelerated change in our society is a challenge to become a new people on a new planet, to celebrate the eruptions in the culture and in our imaginations as indicators of a shift that will take us into a new era in which we can experience oneness with the entire

Earth community. Creativity is our right of passage into an evolutionary consciousness. In the act of creativity, we experience a resurrection of the soul. As a people and a culture, through creativity we heal the hole in our troubled heart. Creativity becomes a practice of courage and conscience. We give expression to the sacred impulse that resides in the imagination and the recesses of our soul.

A Language for the Soul. The poet Rainer Maria Rilke wrote, "Words are the last resort for what lies deep within." The desire to celebrate, to create rituals, lies deep within the human heart. We seek ways to share food and drink, to move and touch, to reflect, and to listen to the wisdom of the ages. We transform eating, bathing, and going about our daily tasks into moments and opportunities of ritual in order to deepen our lives. We see all creation as a sanctuary and every event as an opportunity to celebrate, to remember with gratitude our ancestors, whether relatives, rocks, or the ocean. In viewing the "picture rocks" near Tucson, Arizona, I was in awe of both the pictures on the rocks and the sense of history they convey. Art is ritual that tells our story so that we remember who we are and celebrate who we can become.

Lessons from the Game of Life. Spiritual writers from Meister Eckhart to Gandhi, from Mechtilde to Merton, have consistently reminded us that the capacity for play is central to the spiritual journey. In a culture of management by objectives, planned vacations, and organized athletics for toddlers, authentic play is essential. This is not the ritual of our free-enterprise economy, where "play" is about winning and losing, about vicious competition and astronomical salaries and signing bonuses. Real play is participation in the art of living. It strengthens the body, awakens the mind, and summons us to savor the moment.

CELEBRATING SPIRIT

Diarmuid O'Murchu wrote, "Deep within the human psyche —
at all stages of our evolutionary development — is the power of
Spirit seeking engagement and expression. Deep within creation
itself is the same creative Spirit."

Letting Go. One of the greatest challenges for people today is to
move from the self-enclosed "autistic" ego-self to become cosmic
people. Their pain and struggle are also the energy source for fash-
ioning a planetary community that is vital, compassionate, and
whole. Such an undertaking requires that we face the challenges
before us, realize within ourselves the energy necessary to move
forward, embrace new ideas, and listen to the collective wisdom
that bubbles up within us through the voices of Earth.

In classical theology, this spiritual path that we are being invited to embark upon is known as the *via negativa,* the negative
way. It invites us to give up even denial and to open ourselves to
the struggles of life. This spiritual practice takes us beyond the dark
night of the institutional soul, the dark night of incipient despair
that permeates our psyches, and the dark night of dismantled and
misdirected leadership. To embrace the dark night of our times
is to give up the illusion that we are in control of all dimensions
of our life. To live into the *via negativa* is to allow ourselves to
let go of many of the formational belief systems that we have inherited from our culture and our churches. To let go of a God
who is fixed and distant. To let go of a tradition that claims to
possess all truth and that imposes contradictions on our impulses
and wholesome aspirations. To let go of a historical and static religion that sees incarnation, revelation, and crucifixion as events
frozen in time. To let go of human arrogance and denominational
superiority. To move beyond the inheritance of a world that has re-

pressed our imaginations, fostered conformity, and denied radical restructuring.

Julian of Norwich reminds us that "seeing God cannot be a continuous experience." That is the nature of who we are. Meister Eckhart said, "Only those who let go can dare to reenter." In other words, unless you let go of your marriage, the marriage may not survive. Unless you let go of trying to be the teacher, nobody is going to learn. It's all about letting go and daring to reenter. We are both divine and finite. That is the paradox we are trying to live with. Our lives are marked by what we have let go of: relationships, jobs, places. In our spirituality of letting go, we learn reverence and appreciation. Letting go of illusion makes it possible to grasp what is truly real. In letting go of the enemy, we discover forgiveness. Letting go of self-centeredness and competition uncovers the possibility of gratitude and partnership.

Today we are in a planetary crisis. A few years ago, a child might stand up in school and say, "I'm afraid I'm not going to grow up because they're going to destroy this world with a nuclear bomb." Now the fear of ecological devastation of the planet has replaced the threat of nuclear war. The doorway to planetary peace is ecological awareness. The bomb is no longer a primary threat, but the ecological bomb has already gone off. Our relationship to Earth is imperiled.

I have previously alluded to the cultural earthquake. The planetary community is both collapsing and being born right now. We are all familiar with the long list of environmental ills: the greenhouse effect, the death of the rain forest, toxic waste, topsoil depletion, species extinction, and on and on. Another predictable result of cultural collapse is fundamentalism. Whenever a culture dies, clarity gets lost. Things get muddy. People want answers that do not exist. That is why fundamentalism is so strong in times of cultural transition. It gives the illusion of clarity where it does not exist.

We need to allow the structures to die, whether they are ecclesial, political, educational, or medical. The paschal mystery is being re-enacted in our midst: incarnation and death, but also resurrection. Things die, but life continues.

Compassion. When I first heard of planetary spirituality, the dimension that captured me personally and most touched my energy and interest was its culmination in justice. It was not about climbing a ladder or some kind of pietistic escapism; it was about engaging in life — an engagement I now call geo-justice.

Everything culminates in compassion. Creativity needs criticism. Compassion is the litmus test of an authentic and planetary spirituality; it is the way in which we put some boundaries and judgments on our creativity. Compassion is related to pain, even cosmic pain. In other words, when we extend our awareness of our pain to the pain of Earth, we move into compassion. Then we can channel our creativity. Rabbi Heschel said that "every time someone suffers, God cries." Compassion is, in a very real way, about relieving the pain of God.

Compassion is about healing. Meister Eckhart defined work as "whatever needs to be done." Compassion and justice are about whatever needs to be done. The work of compassion involves celebration. That is why Martin Luther King, Jr., was so powerful. People learned to sing the freedom songs and dance, to be, and to make justice. Whenever there is a connection between art and justice, power is generated. Justice is more than being with other warm bodies. Spirit adds a dimension of celebration to the art of justice. Emma Goldman said, "If I can't dance, I don't want to be part of your parade."

The universe also is involved in the work of compassion. Another way of defining compassion is "balance and harmony in the universe." It is in our deepest nature to live in balance with each other and with all of creation. The practice of compassion joins the event of justice — geo-justice — with celebration.

Compassion is about celebrating our diversity. Not everybody participates in protest marches, not everybody goes to the soup kitchen, not everybody goes to an AIDS hospice, not everybody saves the whales. We are called to our unique dimension of compassion. Justice-making needs to reflect our diversity. Some people need to go to the library, other people need to go to the streets, and yet others need to go to the garden. Compassion is much like being in love. When we experience an attraction, certain things happen. Certain injustices arouse us out of our own pain and woundedness, and then we act. Each of us is aroused to a different act of justice-making. Each of us sees the *anawim* (the biblical word for the poor and voiceless) in a different guise. The planet is the *anawim* of today, and so are women, racial minorities, animals, rain forests, and many others.

Compassion is about a new heart, a new structure, and a new consciousness flowing out of the art of our lives. We connect with each other, with ourselves, with Earth — that's geo-justice. And compassion is about prophecy. Walter Brueggemann talks about prophecy as making a decision about what to tear up and what to plant. In the prophetic act, we leave some things behind, and we take some things with us. The spirituality of Spirit is a prophetic movement because it takes the treasures of our pre-Reformation Western Christian heritage with us while letting other things go. It is totally and deeply ecumenical within the Christian and other Wisdom traditions.

Compassion is not elitist. It is not about pity or "feeling sorry" for others. Its tradition is born out of a shared interdependence and a sense of awe. We live in the fetal waters of cosmic grace. Not only must we celebrate this, but we must struggle for those in our midst who are deeply wounded by poverty of soul and/or body.

Transformation. Teilhard de Chardin wrote the most profound
description of transformation that I have found anywhere:

> I became aware that I was losing contact with myself. And
> each step of the descent a new person was disclosed within
> me of whose name I was no longer sure and who no longer
> obeyed me. And when I had to stop my exploration because
> the path faded beneath my steps, I found a bottomless abyss
> at my feet, and out of it comes arising, I know not from
> where, the current which I dare to call my life.

As we move into the new era, we look back at the historical development of humanity, from the time of the tribal, shamanic era,
when humans were hunters and gatherers; to the Paleolithic time,
when agriculture was begun, and the land and its fruits became do-
mesticated; to the rise of the great civilizations, in which buildings
and architecture flourished; to the postindustrial era of ecological
devastation and the ever-increasing challenge of overpopulation.
We are living at a time when the "dark night" is signified by the
opaqueness within our psyches, the opaqueness of a vocationless
people, the opaqueness of repressed gifts of workers who are neither
challenged nor rewarded.

But the dark night can bring the dawn. In England, during the
Second World War, in order to avoid becoming targets of the air
strikes, people turned off their lights at night. When planes flew
overhead, they were unable to see any sign of light, unable to spot a
target for their bombs. Just after the declaration of peace, a song became popular in Britain, and in fact around the world: "When the
Lights Go On Again All over the World." It seems to me that the
new creation and the challenge before us at this opaque and challenging time require another kind of illumination. In the words of
Teilhard de Chardin, we need "to rediscover fire," to reignite the
spark of the imagination in our psyches and in our souls. Only then

will our new "process cosmology" become incarnate in our midst, as we live a more integrated, mutually enhancing, and imaginative existence.

Only then will the doorway to a planetary spirituality open when we move out of the rubble of a postindustrial era and engage in "a great turning" that opens our future to a new era of awareness and planetary peace.

Only then will we be able to see with new eyes. Steve, a member of Brothers of Earth, remembered the first time he wore glasses. On the way home from the optometrist, he was fascinated by the beauty of the crimson and orange of the fall leaves and luscious red apples that hung on the trees, waiting to be picked.

Only then will we resolve the apparent paradox that shows up in our deep desire for intimacy and contemplation, the desire for relationship and self-disclosure that co-exists with the seemingly contradictory call to contemplation. This challenge for a planetary spirituality is being lived by "urban contemplatives" who search for depth and meaning in the midst of family, work, and contemporary life. After I addressed this question during a workshop in St. Louis, a wife said to her husband, "Now I understand why I sometimes suggest that we have some quiet time, when we're both at home."

Only then will we be able to transcend the apparent divisions of tradition, gender, race, class, and culture and truly come home as a planetary people to a planetary spirituality.

Only then will we be able to discover the personal and social meaning of the universe story and its implications for our lives.

Only then will we be able to be instruments of healing, to return to our origins, and to create a culture that is marked by relationship, difference, and depth — a planetary spirituality of geo-justice that is truly a celebration of Earth, art, and spirit.

REFLECTIONS

EASTER MORNING

Birds sing
Breezes blow
Sun announces the day
Beauty envelops the meadow
New life springs forth with a symphony of Easter
The sweat lodge door lies open to recall the empty tomb,
and resurrection rises once again.

Prayer. Prayer is puzzling. The more I think about it and ponder its meaning, the more convinced I become that prayer is a paradox. It's a dance between looking for God to provide a solution and becoming engaged as fully as possible in creating the solution ourselves. Prayer is the movement from illusion to reality. It's less about changing God's mind than about embracing the reality of our own lives, attuning our psyche and our soul to the reality as life presents itself. Therefore, prayer is more about trust and hope than it is about rearranging the universe on our behalf. We acknowledge that our perceptions and ideas of what is needed — not only in our lives, but for the planet itself — are limited and, of necessity, confined to our own levels of awareness. At the same time, this "passive volition" should not be confused with an exaggerated sense of divine providence that renders us passive and disengaged from the very things that we are called upon to accomplish. St. Ignatius of Loyola counseled, "Work as if everything depends on you, and pray as if everything depends on God." This mantra challenges us to be fully engaged in life while at the same time recognizing that the entire cosmic view is reserved only to the divine. So prayer is not all passive acceptance and not all relentless pursuit of "my way or no way."

There is mounting evidence at the scientific level that prayer "works." Dr. Larry Dossey demonstrated in a project conducted at the University of San Francisco Hospital that people who are prayed for, with all the other variables being equal, healed more quickly than those who are not prayed for.

Prayer requires us to embrace reality, to work toward life, to be open to change, to trust the depths of our wisdom, and to realize our limitations. In prayer we remain open to the unknown, to the hidden wisdom of life's mysteries. Perhaps that is one of life's greatest puzzles.

Meister Eckhart said, "If the only prayer you ever say is 'Thank you,' that is enough." The prayer of gratitude is the prayer of interconnectedness, an acknowledgment that we have had an origin outside ourselves. God does not have a beginning, but everyone and everything else does — in the sense that we all receive life from outside ourselves. We receive everything that we have from outside ourselves. If we live in this universe in an interconnected way, we will feel gratitude. I am always impressed when I meet people who say, "I'm so grateful for my home, for my family, for whatever." Such people feel interconnected and healed of cynicism and self-pity.

Sometimes we need to remind ourselves that we are exactly in the place in our life that we need to be. We can take away the worry of what we are going to do with the rest of our life and deal with what is appropriate for us right now. Whether we feel at a crisis or an oasis in our life, at this moment we are right where we need to be. That is so important. Yet it is common to regret the past and fear the future.

I believe that as we celebrate pleasure we become increasingly aware of the energy of the divine permeating the entire universe. Think for a moment of what it was like before creation. Close your eyes and roll the clock back thirteen billion years to that primordial, pregnant moment when all things began. The energy that flows through us and from us is a continuation of that moment. *We* are a continuation of that moment.

We live at a time of a planetary awakening, when people of all traditions are beginning to reclaim and to celebrate their experience of the divine; to honor their own deepest experience in trust that the markers for their journey will be discovered in their inner promptings and in the events that affect their lives. Such people are increasing their sense of reverence for the entire Earth community. They see life as sacred and recognize the divine presence in and through all existence. In their new knowing, they long for and seek out community, places to discover and create, places of meaning and compassion. With spiritual courage they allow themselves to move beyond old oppressions and search out the avenues that will nourish their psyche and heal their soul. They listen to the New Story with their heart. David Stendl-Rast wrote, "Eyes see only light, ears hear only sound, but a listening heart perceives meaning."

How would Earth speak to us at this particular moment? This is my own imagined "letter from Gaia":

Dear Easter People,

I am grateful for your efforts to do what you can to make life more livable.

I am grateful for your striving to understand how embedded you and all humanity are in the community of life we share together.

I am grateful for your efforts to connect to the cycles of existence that reveal the meaning of birth, death, and rebirth.

I am grateful for your struggle to generate the energy to make life more hopeful, tomorrow more possible, and the memory of those who have gone before brighter.

I am grateful for your wisdom and for your growing awareness of the divine.

I am grateful for your willingness to join the community of life and to celebrate the art of the possible.

I am grateful for your capacity to surrender to the wonder of life and the uncertainty before you, for your willingness to embrace the awesomeness of the universe in your particular bioregion.

May your journey continue, your dreams be realized, and your spirit find fulfillment, as the story continues to unfold.

Love,
Gaia

As the spirit of Easter expands, I am reminded of a practice that I first encountered in Rochester, New York. Later it was practiced in Toronto, and today I am sure it happens in many centers. We called it the Secular Stations of the Cross. The practice involved visiting or reenacting events in which oppression ("crucifixions") occur in our time. The stations might include a bank, representing the temple of those who invest in oppressive regimes; a laboratory where nuclear warheads are researched and made; or an underdeveloped country with an oppressed people — say, the Philippines during the Marcos era. We need to ask where crucifixion is happening *now*. Where are our temples? What powers do we worship? What forces impinge upon us? What evils invite our participation? To what forces do we pay homage?

Sunrise, flowers, spring, newness, surprise, the empty tomb — all these are analogies for Easter. Easter is the affirmation of hope that tomorrow can be different from today. Easter is mystery. Easter is all that we strive for. We await its coming.

Thomas Merton wrote of how we must face the challenge of how prayer can become a source of collaboration rather than division when he wrote: "We are going to have to create a new language of prayer. And this new language of prayer has to come out of something which transcends all our traditions, and comes out of the immediacy of love."

Always in the Beginning. There is magic in something new. As a boy growing up in Sombra, Ontario, Canada, a village of three hundred people nestled on the banks of the St. Claire River, I remember spring. Sap would run from the big maple tree in our backyard. The snow would melt; the ice would begin to flow in the river and disappear in the channel. Spring was a wonderful time of many new beginnings.

In recent years, I have been moved by other beginnings. Each year at the Sophia Center, my colleagues and I welcome a new group of students. There is a magic in the air. People of different genders, races, traditions, bioregions, and ages enter a room and discover an incredible connection through their common concern for Earth and every species. This moment becomes a new beginning of community and friendship. Energy is generated, hope restored, and possibilities made palpable. It seems unmistakably true that life is a series of beginnings in which each resurrection moment is a unique opportunity to savor and embrace existence in its most exalted form.

Intimacy and Contemplation. Just as there is a quest for contemplation, there is also a desire for intimacy, a quest to experience meaningful relationship. Intimacy—a fully embodied connectedness—is a challenge for both single and married. Intimacy is more than presence; it is a soul connection, fully felt, mystical moments that connect us to our selves, to others, to the universe and the divine. Intimacy is a work of the heart, an experience of communion, a time of being enveloped in the energy of the "curvature of compassion" that holds the entire cosmos in a loving embrace.

Upon deeper reflection, we can discover that in the silence of "the contemplative moment" resides a palpable union with self, other, and all that is. Also as we penetrate the silence we discover both the intimacy and contemplation. We discover oneness: together the paradox of apparent appositives become a unifying principle of the whole.

CHILEAN CREED

I believe that behind the mist the sun waits.
I believe that beyond the dark night it is raining stars.
I believe in secret volcanoes and the world below.
I believe that this lost ship will reach port.
They will not rob me of hope,
it shall not be broken.
it shall not be broken,
My voice is filled to overflowing
with the desire to sing,
the desire to sing.

I believe in reason, and not in force of arms.
I believe that peace will be sown throughout the earth.
I believe in our nobility, created in the image of God,
and with free will reaching for the skies.
They will not rob me of hope,
it shall not be broken,
it shall not be broken.

THE INTEGRAL PROCESS

Such a metanoic shift from materialism to spirituality, further-more, has been taking place on our microcosmic scale through-out the individual lives of a number of significant minds of the twentieth century, people whose work is contributing to the death of the mechanical worldview and who are taking spirituality seriously.   —JOHN DAVID EBERT

Seeing

~ Reflect on your experience of God (the divine in your life).

~ How is your story one of new awareness, depth, meaning, purpose, and destiny?

~ What gives you strength, energy, and psychic power with hope and zest?

Judging

~ What does your spirituality reveal to you about the depths of your life journey and the place of change and possibility in your life?

~ What wise people energize your life and deepen your spiritu-ality?

~ What concrete experiences of awe, pain, creativity, and com-passion alter the landscape of your soul and encourage you to take up life's challenges?

Acting

- ~ Choose specific spiritual practices to "grow your soul" and deepen your spirituality. (For example, spend time with nature, meditate silently, engage in direct contact with the poor, develop ecological practices.)

- ~ Become more aware of the needs of your body (e.g., for food, exercise, and rest).

- ~ Reflect on ways to enhance your self-awareness, your self-expression, your and relationships.

Good is everything that brings a spiritual growth to the world. Best is what assures the highest development of the spiritual powers of the Earth. —Pierre Teilhard de Chardin

Chapter Five

Recognizing Our Origins

When religious reflection today opens its door to the natural world, it is met with a wondrous array of insights.

— Elizabeth Johnson

Through reflecting on our roots, we experience mystery and become conscious that each moment is an incident of divine disclosure. We shed light on our traditions, and we discover fresh connections between what we deeply trust is true and new possibilities for action in every area of our lives.

Throughout history, spiritual movements and communities have taken up the challenge to purify the culture and render it more functional. The monastic orders are one example. Thomas Merton compared a monk to a tree: as a tree converts carbon dioxide into oxygen, the monk purifies the toxic culture. Many orders took up this task through preaching, health care, and education. More recent expressions of this trend include Alcoholics Anonymous and other Twelve-Step groups, back-to-the-land movements, and "green monasteries," with their Earth literacy and community-supported agriculture programs.

Each of these movements of cultural transformation compels us to examine our tradition. Just as St. Thomas Aquinas reflected theologically on the philosophy of Aristotle, we are being asked today to reflect on the new cosmology that is emerging from the discoveries of quantum physics, evolutionary science, the creation stories of indigenous peoples, and the mystics of Christianity and other world religions. This challenge requires us to embark on a new adventure that is deeply felt, ecological, and purposeful.

One approach to achieving the new synthesis is the practice of *theological reflection.* In this process, we discover our "operative theology," that is, the connection between our deepest sacred impulses and the root convictions of our traditions. The result is a healing of the separation between our "deep knowing" and our theology. Doing theology in this way assists us to experience mystery; we experience the divine by becoming conscious that each moment of our lives is revelatory. Theology becomes more about consciousness than about analysis and ideology. Theological reflection in geo-justice opens us to an operative theology of Earth, a gospel view that sees the planet as the poor, the voiceless, and the locus of divine action.

Through theological reflection, we learn to trust our imagination as we apply our experiences of protest and self-discovery to the concrete circumstances of our lives. Theological reflection aligns faith and life; it brings to the surface an intuitive value system that gives meaning, energy, and purpose.

Such an approach is responsive both to our experience and to the needs of Earth. It sheds new light on our traditions, releases fresh energy, and encourages us to discover possibilities for action in every area of our life. It prevents us from uncritically accepting imposed patterns of living and acting. It also challenges ways that religion can be used to sanction the status quo whether it be the Gulf War, the bombing of Kosovo, political asylum for a Cuban child, or a variety of other issues. Our theological reflections can reveal the imbalances on the planet and lead to prophetic impulses that demand concrete action. Through connecting these reflections with the gospel, we develop an operative theology of Earth.

Several years ago, when I was at the Toronto School of Theology, we organized what we called theological reflection groups. The result was the discovery of each person's operative theology — the deep connections that exist between our outer action in the world and what we most deeply believe and trust as true. When this congruence takes place, something profound happens. New energy is released. Liberation theologians call this orthopraxis (as opposed to orthodoxy).

When this alignment takes place, participants experience a new sense of joy, harmony, and effectiveness in their lives. This could be compared to what happens when one turns on a water tap or a light switch. No longer is there a dichotomy between what we believe and how we live.

Ultimately, theological reflection is a particular act of prayer. It occurs when we are able to remove any illusion or false consciousness from our lives and to embrace reality in the fullest way possible. In so doing, we open ourselves to the dynamics of the universe and make it possible to come to terms with the challenges of our lives, whether disappointment, anger, fear, or loss. We achieve a deep experience of peace, a renewed confidence, as we move forward knowing that our actions are aligned to the depths of our tradition, our personal convictions, and the unfolding dynamics of the universe itself.

Our spiritual journey is evolutionary, holistic, and mystical. Spirituality actuates the imagination, calls upon courage, and demands openness as we strive for affirmation and action. The spiritual journey leads to liberation, feminism, a new economics, participatory politics, and ecological sensitivity. At this time of transition, the spiritual quest is marked by a profound interconnectedness between humans and the other-than-human world, the entire Earth community. A spirituality that flows out of the New Story and that is deeply integrated into the practice of justice-making fosters hope and supports creativity.

A Paschal Mystery for Our Time

Matthew Fox wrote, "In a Cosmic Christ context, the paschal mystery takes on new power, deep meaning, and moral passion.... It is then the life, death, and resurrection of Mother Earth."

The paschal mystery finds its origin in the dynamic unfolding of Jesus' incarnation, crucifixion, and resurrection, leading toward Pentecost. In our time, the paschal mystery embraces a meaning that is more expansive than previously imagined. The incarnation can be understood within the radical inclusiveness of the New Creation Story as the genesis of Earth and every species. The story includes a punctuated equilibrium, the deep dynamic of creation and destruction that Jesus himself engaged in and, today, as the Cosmic Christ, acts out in and through the cosmos itself.

This incarnational energy continues to emerge, give birth, and unfold. Each new moment of time, each fresh event of creation, becomes and continues to become an incarnational moment, a sacred event of newness and birth, an event in which we are all bathed in the energy and newness of the divine. At this critical juncture in human Earth history, we are called to respond to the questions, Where is Bethlehem today? Where is new life taking place? Where is the imagination active? Where is birth happening? Where is there an eruption of fresh energy? What is happening in our culture, which stands at the precipice of new ideas, institutions, projects, programs, relationships, and more? How is the cosmos continuing to find expression in the "microcosmos" of our lives?

The paschal mystery for our time names the cross as a cosmic crucifixion, a crucifixion that is marked by the death of the rain forest, the extinction spasms of species, the irretrievable loss of top-soil and old-growth forests, the melting of the Arctic ice cap, the proliferation of terminal illnesses like AIDS, cancer, and heart disease, and the hole in the ozone layer. Regarding the last, a student from Australia reported that in her school the children were not allowed to go outside at recess unless they wore a wide-brimmed hat or played under a tent — a tragic testimony to the thinning of the ozone layer and the accompanying threat of cancer. Yet death is also evolutionary and organic. Through the entropic cycles of life, we die into Earth and enter the cyclical process ourselves as participants of a new genesis and return. The cosmic crucifixion is both the result of human greed and a distortion of the trajectory toward new life. In this time of devastation and loss, there can be death without resurrection — as understood in the premature extinction of species. Death can also be a prelude to new life, as when grass fires lead to new growth or volcanic eruptions prepare new land.

Making our Easter with Earth names the resurrection moments that envelop our lives and show up on the planet. Resurrection happens! In the larger cycles of death and return, newness emerges from the cross. As a tree flourishes with fresh fruit after pruning, or a child gains renewed appreciation for health after an illness, or the poor discover joy even in the face of death and abject poverty, we learn again and again that the cross is not the end of the story. "Making our Easter" reveals to us that there is life after death. In fact, life exists *within* apparent death. *Easter,* then, is the most important word that we can utter. Our New Story and the cosmology that gives it voice consistently remind us that the cross will always and inevitably redound to new life, however hidden or opaque our vision may be.

A planetary Pentecost emerges with the infusion of a new reciprocity and mutuality between humans and the entire Earth community. A planetary Pentecost becomes the culmination of the paschal mystery. Its completion leads once again to new creation and new life. It is a way of being in the world—a context in which hope is born, our lives flourish, and fresh and meaningful relationships are fostered through a new vision. A planetary Pentecost happens through relationship and interconnectedness, when all creation experiences harmony, balance, and peace; when the original fireball erupts in our psyches and is revealed in the events of our day; and when, through the reign of geo-justice, we have discovered a new world order of love, liberation, and compassion.

RECOVERING THE SACRED

Elizabeth Johnson wrote, "We need to appreciate all over again that the whole universe is a sacrament, vivified by the energy of the Creator Spirit present in all creation as its very animation. The Spirit effects the redemption of both languishing vines and brokenhearted merry makers: that is, the Spirit's presence is for all species."

I remember the "benchmarks" of my tradition: the sacraments of initiation, baptism, confirmation, and communion. However, I now realize that my childhood was shaped and focused in powerful ways by what today I call the primary sacrament of creation.

As I think back over the years, I realize that my conscious encounters with the divine were the experience of beauty and enchantment with the St. Clair River, the comforting shade of the stately maple in our backyard, and the generous bounty of my father's garden. I recall the rain on the roof in the evenings; the pickerel and perch that jumped from the water at dawn or dusk; the sunsets; the snow that carpeted our small village in winter; and the gold, orange, and red leaves that adorned the trees each fall. All of these and more made up my primary sacrament of initiation, my encounter with the divine.

These moments of enchantment and beauty — sometimes stark, but more often awesome — introduced me to the sacred and passed on the promise of exaltation. What I learned then and understand more deeply now is that the rain, leaves, vegetables, snow, river, fish, and breezes reveal to me the nature of the divine, not through words, but through the senses. To be aware of this divine communication is the true invitation to which each of us is called.

This experience of the sacred from our beginning years continues to influence and animate our lives. The recovery of the sacred has profound implications not just for us as individuals but for human-planetary relations. Having inherited a theology that overemphasized transcendence, we have lost sight of the experience of the divine in all things. This absence of the sacred has made possible the devastation of our planet and the abuse of the body — and the body politic as well.

To recover a sense of the sacred is to reclaim an incarnational theology, in which Earth, humanity, and all that is becomes ever-renewing, good, and beautiful. Through recovering a sense of the sacred, we realize that we are born into blessing. We reclaim the original goodness that marinates our soul and realize from our depths that the divine is present in all of life. To recover a sense of the sacred is to realize that we are "all bathed in God," that we are created in wholeness, and that our lives are destined for joy and celebration.

As we return to our origins, we realize that we are the continuation in space and time of that original outburst of energy and divine generosity. We embrace the wisdom of all traditions and acknowledge the divine communication that is revealed to us in each moment. To recover a sense of the sacred is to experience the primacy of joy, the depth of goodness, and the power of silence. We realize that the entire Earth community is being created and re-created moment by moment as a source of healing, celebration, and justice-making.

To recover a sense of the sacred is to realize that within our inmost depths lies the energizing force that can lead to a compassionate embrace of all of life. The entire cosmos, humanity included, is genetically coded for the creation of compassion. To recover the sacred is to develop receptivity and a listening heart and to rediscover the sacramentality of human experience — in fact, the sacramentality of Earth itself. We recover the sacred as we acknowledge the wisdom of John Shea, who reminded us that "the mystery in which we are held is fundamentally benign."

Option for the Poor — and Poor Earth

Leonard Boff wrote: "The starting point must also be redefined, namely, the option for the poor, including the most threatened beings in creation. The first of these is Planet Earth as a whole." Building on liberation theology's preferential option for the poor, geo-justice challenges us to a preferential option for Earth. This option invites us into a practical solidarity with the wounds of the planet. In the struggle for global justice, we view the world itself as victim. The world is hungry, sick, and dying. A preferential option for Earth calls us to a theology rooted in the experience of global oppression, ecological devastation, and institutionalized resistance to social, gender, political, and economic equality. We see ourselves as one with the raped rain forests, abused children, marginalized women, and economically disadvantaged peoples everywhere. We embrace our experience of interconnectedness and solidarity with the poor and with poor Earth. We awaken to the needs of the biosphere.

The option for the poor is based on the conviction that the divine is most present within and among the poor — that indeed "the last shall be first." Through the option for the poor, the most radically excluded become the model for radical inclusion. To reflect on our lives and to respond deeply from this perspective is of great importance. Our response may be one of active engagement and service or profound reflection on the causes and consequences of poverty. The option for the poor demands that we simplify our lifestyle, that we "live simply that others may simply live."

We are called to a preferential option for Earth, which is sacred, divine, and the body of Christ in our time. To respond to a preferential option for Earth, to practice geo-justice, is to heal the cultural tendencies that separate society from the planet and the social from the ecological. A preferential option for Earth fosters a renewed sense of the sacredness of each member of the community of life. As our attention shifts toward poor Earth, we become increasingly aware that the power of the poor available to us for restoration and renewal is also available within Earth itself. This option for Earth invites us into a life of practical solidarity with the wounded ones, the *anawim* of every species.

As we open ourselves to the beauty and brokenness of our time, we experience the presence of the divine and are moved to respond in a manner that includes the interest and awareness of all members of the Earth's community.

A NEW EXODUS MOMENT

Thomas Berry wrote, "We are in the present time in an Exodus moment. This Exodus is a journey of Earth entire. Hopefully we will make the transition successfully."

Liberation theology places its emphasis on action to transform the world. Out of this comes our knowledge of the divine. Put another way, reflection begins after action. The themes of liberation find their scriptural sources in Exodus and the writings of the prophets, who denounced injustice and spoke out in solidarity with the poor.

The Exodus motif integrates liberation and planetary theology. This story of transformation and deliverance of the people of Israel is a precursor of two crucial approaches to freedom and fulfillment in our time: the personal and the planetary, which are in fact one. Leonardo Boff underscored this point when he wrote, "The notion is growing that any attack on Earth is aggression against the sons and daughters of Earth."

Liberation theology encourages people to move away from internalized oppression; that is, because of unresolved psychological issues, we live as if the system is within us. In fact, we oppress ourselves, interiorizing racial, gender, or class injustices. Liberation theology also confronts the external systems of oppression, the structures of society and culture that promote bias and inequality among people. Finally, liberation theology evokes an Exodus moment that heals any distance in our relationship with the divine. Through theological reflection, we explore the contradictions between our unjust world and a world of justice and peace.

Planetary theology is about designing a path toward freedom, that occurs when we make the transition from the end of the current era in Earth history (the Cenozoic era) and move toward a new era in human Earth history (the Ecozoic era). From the perspective of planetary spirituality, the entire planet is making the Exodus. At the same time, humanity is growing increasingly intolerant of a worldview that has guided our lives toward destruction. This great Exodus must move in the direction of a cultural healing that will flow from a new understanding of the origin, structure, and unfolding of the universe and of our particular place within it. Planetary theology proposes that this practice of a preferential option for Earth will result in a mutually enhancing relationship between the human and the other-than-human worlds.

The universe (and therefore everyone and everything) is in a state of genesis. We are moving forward today toward an integral approach that incorporates the insights and prophetic vision and practice of both liberation theology and creation theology. Only through the practice of a planetary spirituality will we realize a new synthesis between the human and other-than-human worlds, between creation and liberation, between North and South, between the social and the ecological, between people and the planet.

Gustavo Gutiérrez, the pioneer architect of liberation theology, wrote, "Creation is the first act of liberation." This assertion collapses the separation between culture, humanity, and Earth. In fact, it reminds us that *all* members of the Earth community have an inner drive to fulfill the purpose of their existence and the freedom necessary to carry out their journey. At this nexus of creation and liberation theologies reside the freedom and fulfillment of our converging journeys — a planetary spirituality.

Theological reflection through the lens of the new cosmology provokes fresh insights into our faith, traditions, and the life questions that confront us:

~ Where did we come from?

~ What is our destiny?

~ What is the nature of the divine?

~ How does the New Story reflect reality?

~ How does tradition interact with the new science?

~ In what way does the power of story enhance our passion for living?

REFLECTIONS

Wisdom and a Listening Heart. When I was a child, my Aunt Margaret would occasionally speak of certain people as "old souls." I think what she meant was that some people have a comprehension of life that far surpasses their years or their level of formal study. Aunt Margaret was talking about wisdom. For her, and now for me, a wise person is someone who can deal with the realities of everyday life, who is capable in finding the depth of existence in the still, small moments of daily living.

As a teenager, I was deeply engaged in baseball, even entertaining hopes for a while to play professionally. My brother and I often spent our Sunday afternoons with our friend and baseball coach, Roy Tennyson. We sat for hours in his home or under the tree in his backyard, listening to him talk. Sometimes he would listen for hours to us. I think it was under that apple tree that I connected wisdom with a listening heart.

When Agendas Collide. Accountability is a watchword in the workplace. Organizations demand that we "go along with the system." In the process, as Saul Alinsky said, the organizations "oppose their original purpose." They attempt to protect themselves from the cleansing process of self-examination and transformative change. Institutions, in fact, almost invariably develop an agenda that is geared to their survival rather than to the fulfillment of their original purpose.

People are often victims of the same phenomenon. They may seem to have firm convictions on the major issues of life — for example, politics, race, gender, and ecology — yet, when confronted with choices, they abandon their convictions. They "talk the talk," but they don't "walk the walk." They leave their politics at the door.

Paulo Freire said that we all have contradictions in our lives.

Clearly, there is often disparity between what we proclaim and what we practice. A key area of contradiction is the disparity between our personal values and the values of the structures with which we associate, whether social, cultural, economic, religious, or political. The resolution of these inevitable contradictions is found in our personal conscience, which should take priority when two agendas collide.

Living on the Edge of Death. An old monk was asked, "What would you do if you knew you were going to die in a few days?" The monk answered, "I would go on doing as I'm doing now."

Would that be *your* response? Are there things you've neglected doing until you "have the time"? Are you engaged in activities or relationships that you would rather end? To live as though you're dying — and you are! — is both a challenge and an invitation. What would you celebrate? Lament? Change?

After the darkness and the sleep of winter, we see the world coming alive in our eyes. Which of us has not taken delight at the first sight of delicate snowdrops swaying in the breeze or newborn lambs playing in the field...? We are the present custodians of this ancient land.... The loss of even one species diminishes the richness of the landscape. It also represents a fading out of one unique creature in the wonderful tapestry of God's creation.... In their search for God, the monks were guided by two books, the Bible and the Book of Nature. God speaks in a special way to those who have ears to listen, eyes to see, and hearts to respond to the few areas of relative wilderness which have survived.

— SEAN McDONAUGH

The Integral Process

Today an integrative theology is being developed. There are many factors that contribute to the renaissance. The biblical renewal of recent years has taught us to see that creation and the capacity for liberation are what we have in common. An appreciation of native/indigenous religions is also making possible a new integration: we have discovered their ancient wisdom as a source of mystery and a renewed respect for the power of the seasons, the creator, and the Earth. We are also being united on a common journey by the emergence of the women's movement. This new experience of inclusiveness and oneness has profound implications for understanding the divine, religion, spirituality, humanity, and Earth.

Another significant factor in the spiritual renaissance is the realization that justice is constitutive to the gospel; the development of liberation theology and the annunciation of the preferential option for the poor by the Latin American bishops further amplified the unifying principle of justice. With these reflections, we began to realize that the "Cry of the Poor" and the "Cry of the Earth" were one voice, and were in fact the voice of God.

> Enthusiasm is a certain joy in living like that which comes over us when we have discovered something entirely new and ask ourselves how it was ever possible to live without this for so long. It is as though it were something that had been latent in us, awaiting the proper moment to appear. —Paulo Freire

Seeing

~ How do your spirituality and theological tradition either support or thwart your impulse toward a full and creative life?

~ Some would say that Western Christianity fosters morality before mysticism. What is your response to this statement?

~ Others suggest that liturgical celebrations often result in a deep disappointment for the participants — that is, they feel a discrepancy between what is symbolized (e.g., in the Eucharist) and what is actually experienced. Do you feel a congruence between your sacred impulses and the understanding of your tradition and its teachings?

Judging

~ How is it possible to heal the discrepancy between what you deeply know is true and the ethical teachings of your tradition?

~ As you survey the key questions in your life, what is your "operative theology"?

Acting

~ Decide to take appropriate steps to heal the division between your actions in the world and your deep beliefs.

If you can't have empathy with the suffering people, if you are not capable of understanding deep within, it is better to retire from existence. — PAULO FREIRE

To reflect theologically on a spiritual experience means to work through it by relating it to the thinking of one's age, and the other ways of understanding the following of Jesus.

— GUSTAVO GUTIÉRREZ

Chapter Six

A Story of Hope

It's now only dawn.
— Pope John XXIII

The autumn season flared in red, orange, and gold as we gathered at the Springbank Renewal Center, located in the poorest district of the United States: Williamsburg County, South Carolina. We came to this place that was previously occupied by Native Americans, which now houses a cemetery mostly occupied by slaves. The Center practices indigenous wisdom through sweat lodges, pipe ceremonies, and vision quests. It is a home for artists and for others who wish to transform the landscapes of their souls. A "grandmother tree" stands stately on the lawn, viewing the frolicking puppies, the pond, and the woods. Our group included young families and grandparents; engineers, therapists, animal lovers, and administrators; Catholics, Protestants, seekers, and the unchurched. We came to rediscover the fire in our lives — to deepen our understanding of love, relationship, and our primary connections to creation. Our aim was to examine our roots, tell stories of our ancestors, and reflect on how, as a people, we would like to be remembered. We planned to celebrate our tradition, share a simple meal of bread and wine, and relax with music, movement, and song.

We came to find community, to be healed from loneliness, and to discover new companions on the way. Moved by the sight of a deer, the song of a bird, and the promptings of our own hearts, we explored the options that lay before us. We came for a weekend, and we returned home with a renewed capacity to look forward to a fruitful life.

On Community

We all want to be with people to whom we do not have to explain ourselves. We ask ourselves: Where do I find a context to continue my journey? Where do I find community? We know intuitively that we can do together what we could never do alone. We experience a deep desire for interconnectedness and an increased capacity to ingest the mystery and beauty of the universe. We yearn for a place to "grow" our hearts, making them bigger, more open to beauty, and more courageous in danger. Cosmologists often ask, What time is it in the universe? I think one of the responses to that question is that it is time for community, time to be together — common people, with a common vision, on a common journey.

What is community? Dan Berrigan has said that we "live in an anti-trinitarian culture," a world that denies diversity, supports separation, and represses our inner voice. Community is just the opposite. Community is a trinitarian experience, because it is all about connections and diversity. Thomas Merton once said, "I never felt more in community with my brother monks than when I was alone with them in the monastery." He was talking about a shared vision, a palpable experience of being at one.

Community is the context for the journey from the desert of devastation and alienation to the promised land of ecological balance and personal intimacy. It is the precondition for peace and the basis for solidarity. But community is also about being diverse.

We are "coded" within our genetic makeup as human beings to build community, but we don't all do it the same way. Communities are a celebration of uniqueness, individual paragraphs in the New Story. Building community is like making a quilt: we all have our own patch; yet a common thread unites us.

Our Capacity to See

There was a young man who was blind. He and a friend were taking a guided tour of the Grand Canyon. They stood together at a guard rail with the canyon spread out before them. The sighted man looked all around, saw an airplane, and was distracted by the other people on the tour. But the blind man focused intently on the canyon. "Isn't it beautiful?" he said softly. "Isn't it beautiful?"

The blind man had the capacity to take in what the world offered. Such sensitivity is also involved in building community. We must listen to our inner voices and the voices of others. When I was training as a community organizer, I learned that a meeting has a linear agenda. But we don't build community that way in the new cosmology. Fritjof Capra reminds us that the order is not to be imposed, but will be established by the system itself. Each community is unique. There is no hierarchy, no central location from which to give orders or carry out agendas. Instead, there is an invitation to spontaneity, diversity, and interconnectedness. The gospel of growing a community is based on three things: support, information, and common action. A community is a place to continue the journey; it is not a destination.

What happens in a community? We tell stories: our own story, cultural stories, and the cosmic story. We feel not only the support and wisdom of each other but of the universe itself.

We can picture community as a seed. The communities we are building today are being planted in the darkness, the dark night of injustice of a culture in crisis. But the seeds are being planted in the fertile hearts of people who want connections to grow, who revere diversity, and who listen.

The most powerful image I have of community is as a cosmic fire-web. It is strong around the edges and almost transparent in the center. It glows with the fires of passion and undiminished hope. It is circular because not only do we find our place in our community, but our community is the setting in which we find our place in the universe itself.

As we build our communities, as we celebrate the beauty that we have experienced in stories, in song, in people, and in beautiful places, we realize that community — and spirituality, for that matter — is about hospitality. That's what communities are about. They are places where we are welcomed, cosmically and personally. Carl Jung was fond of saying, "The dream drives the action." It is in community that the work of geo-justice is born and nurtured.

THE DAWNING OF A MOVEMENT

Planetary spirituality moves people toward a holistic worldview. From our dying culture, we draw the fire of knowledge that comes from the heart that fuels us with mysticism and prophecy for our continuing journey.

Planetary spirituality gives birth to our fondest hopes for the planet. These hopes provide a window of opportunity for a truly global network and for a process that will utilize and integrate existing networks as partners in a Pentecost for the planet.

The first task for leaders of this global event will be to develop imaginative ways to translate the vision of planetary spirituality into the lives of all people on Earth. We are called to create a tapestry of relationships, the cosmic fire-web mentioned above. Such a community will give cultural expression to the dynamics of the universe by being autonomous, interconnected, and self-organizing.

Most of us view what happens to us as having significance only in our own lives. We need a perspective that sees both personal and cultural events as expressions of the dynamics of the universe itself. We need to develop a cosmological imagination. I believe that the beginning of this transformation is already happening all around the world. Informal networks of information, support, and common action are springing up. They share a vision, and they often work together toward common goals. The development of these informal "nonorganizations" is transforming how we see life and Earth.

Through these networks, these nonorganizations, we are developing a new window on the world, a new way of seeing and acting in the world. This movement ushers in a new era, a conscious shift toward peace with the planet. Action programs aligned with geo-justice principles are being developed. In-depth reflection is occurring.

The *Toronto Globe and Mail* said that the birth of a movement "resembles nothing so much as the coming of spring; suddenly, spontaneously, everywhere the sap is rising, the trees and buds are swelling." This movement for peace with Earth emerges from a common vision and the diversity of concrete action.

Bioregionally based communities provide a vehicle for bringing about a critical mass of people moving from separation to oneness and empowerment. As they link, a growing number of peacemakers will discover increased harmony within and balance without. Through analysis, strategy, and action, these groups focus on peace with Earth.

This movement encompasses the whole Earth. Through it, Earth is becoming an "organism of oneness." The animators of this awakening are people who grow organically from their own history and traditions. They are willing to be seen, in the words of Gregory Baum and Duncan Cameron, as "far out, marginalized from seats of power, idealistic, irresponsible, naïve, or at least ahead of their time."

As we reflect on the signs of the times, we will see how each of us can contribute to this framework of hope. Because geo-justice does not depend on "power over" but on cooperation, geo-justice is increasingly a pursuit of peace and an experience of oneness. In the words of James Bevel, "A movement is when people live what they sing about." Geo-justice is an affirmation of those words.

When we look at the world through the lens of geo-justice, we see the goal of a global community, although not all the steps along the way. To reach that goal, we must walk through the labyrinth of our own narrowness, sometimes unable to perceive more than one step at a time, trusting that we shall eventually emerge with a renewed consciousness and vision. The challenge comes in letting go of those areas that imprison our imaginations, that lock away our creativity, that prevent us from rising out of our ruts.

As we explore and express our participation in geo-justice as members of a movement and creators of a window for the world, we recognize our need for resources for our journey. These resources include:

- *Personal links.* In the "nonorganization" model, these links start with the individual, who communicates with others. Through reflection and action together, groups can further the growth of geo-justice. These spontaneous activities can be focused through a "views letter" that provides personal information about gifts and needs and is a vehicle for a growing articulation of the theory and practice of geo-justice.

- *Resource centers.* Such centers provide support and serve as places where written and recorded resources can be generated and exchanged. Geo-justice workers can gather at such centers, share their work, and develop programs for others. Some centers already exist.

- *Responsible action.* Participants in the movement are encouraged to respond as individuals, as a group, and in cooperation with other like-minded people to lend and receive support. They benefit from one another's experiences.

An Emerging Vision

In 1962, Pope John XXIII stood at St. Paul's Outside the Walls in Rome and convoked the historic Vatican Council II. In 1963, Martin Luther King, Jr., stood on the steps of the Lincoln Memorial and proclaimed his now historic "I Have a Dream" speech. Today, as we stand at the portals of a new civilization, we search for the vision that will carry us into the transformative times that await us. Together, we gather to name the vision that is emerging from the creative outpouring of the new civilization about to be born.

Emerging from the new civilization is a prophetic mysticism that manifests itself in alternative ways of living, an ecology that encourages us to place our trust in the "commandments of creation," as proposed by Thomas Berry:

You shall remove all poison from the air.
You shall cease all pollution of the water.
You shall cease any contamination of Earth.
You shall be open to the life-giving radiance of the sun.
You shall support the self-sustaining forces of the universe.

One view of our hoped-for future is nourished by the wisdom of the new cosmology and Earth literacy being developed by Berry.

Guided by a vision of a time of creativity for both the human and Earth communities, Berry looks toward an era when a new realization of the sacredness of life will be fostered, accepted, and protected by humankind. He posits the following assumptions about the Earth community:

> The universe is a communion of subjects, not a collection of objects.
>
> Earth exists and can survive only in its integral functioning.
>
> Earth is a one-time endowment.
>
> Earth is primary, and humans are derivative.
>
> There is a single Earth community.

Humans can understand fully and respond effectively to our role in this new era when we understand that our culture has

> oppressed our psyches and colonized our souls;
>
> robbed us of our bodies, dominated women, and devastated the Earth;
>
> institutionalized oppression that has brought society to the doorway of its own death; but it has also
>
> brought us to the threshold of a new vision of hope.

BECOMING A PLANETARY PEOPLE

There is a growing number of embryonic groups who find their inspiration in the New Story and who are striving for the "great turning" that will usher in the ecological era that many of us anticipate. Clearly, something new is emerging in our midst: a new way of understanding the problems that confront us, a new consciousness that will make the future brighter and more hopeful. At this moment, we stand at the dawn of a new day and welcome the birth of a movement.

This movement is tender, vulnerable, and new. Rather than a vehicle of service, it is an organism of oneness and diversity, an energetic impulse of the new creation being born from the unfolding energy of the universe, the continuation of that first eruptive moment, the origin of all our existence.

The great work we are called to do is to be catalytic participants in creating the new world that awaits us. As we participate in the dawn of a new day, we gather with friends to deepen and integrate our experience. We pledge to break the harmful patterns of the past through paying attention, expressing gratitude through an open and courageous heart, and moving forward each day with conscious acts of kindness and compassion that foster life, love, and integrity. We remember our dreams and tell our stories to evoke once again creativity and intimacy. Our movement will be energized by truth-telling and stories, sacrifice and silence. Together we will experience inspiration, take up the challenge, be delighted by life's surprises, and remain flexible and open to the transforming power of love.

It will be a nonhierarchical movement that is based on sharing and community, and it will energize our common struggle. It will be a movement marked by a transformation of consciousness and the empowerment of each participant to act with a new capacity for love. This love is deeply enveloped in the divine mystery, out of which is emerging a new coalition of nongovernmental organizations that work for the liberation of Earth, labor, women, the poor, and others, and that remind us that relatedness is the constitutive pattern of life. There is a groundswell of spontaneous support for a global justice that is rising to arrest the toxic impact of a global capitalism propagated by the World Trade Organization, the World Bank, and the International Monetary Fund that endangers the health of humanity and all ecosystems on our planet.

The dawn of our new movement is a cultural and cosmic breakthrough. Together we will be joined on the journey by others who are also willing to love, do good, succeed, be honest, build, help, and give their best to Earth and every species.

As the future unfolds, we will gather with others, acknowledge our interdependence, and provide encouragement. Only then will we be able to hold on to what is good and to welcome the dawn of our new movement with hope.

Yes! Something new is being born. It is now already dawn: the time for a new vision, a new energy, and a new hope.

A CANTICLE OF HOPE

At this time, we are called to ignite a new meaning of hope. It is a time of expectation and perseverance.

A time of relationship and listening to the wisdom that resides in the recesses of our souls.

A time when through new moments of self-expression our imagination erupts and the divine becomes present in our lives.

A time when the inward search activates an increased momentum toward meaning and purpose in our lives.

A time when we gather to celebrate the traditions of indigenous peoples and the sacred stories of oppressed peoples everywhere.

A time to be aware of an emerging sacramentality being born in the minds and hearts of scientists throughout the world.

A time to reflect on a new cosmology that invites us to ponder the unfolding of the universe and humanity's place within it.

A time to "appreciate nature as a promise rather than a perfection."

A time to evoke positive energy; experience passion, pain, and joy; respond with integrity and unbridled potential.

A time of great expectations and yearnings for a future of promise and peace for the whole community of life.

A time to acknowledge the mystery of systemic change through an increased awareness that it is the divine that prays through us.

A time to respond to the desire for a global movement as we break down barriers and work for change.

A time to ponder the wisdom that comes to us from within a resacralized world that resonates with an inner sense of trust.

A time to foster a listening heart that rediscovers the divine presence in the poor of every species.

A time to embrace vulnerability, to be touched by the pain of the planet and the shimmering beauty of a bud about to flower.

A time to encourage the prophetic voice and support the formation of an ecological consciousness.

A time to embrace ambiguity and foster a dialectical awareness that will result in creativity and a hope-filled future.

A time to face our fears and take whatever risks are necessary to discover community and experience belonging.

A time to trust the depth of our deepest convictions that they may move us out of the "comfort zone" of our existing community and into a new context yet to be formed.

A time to realize that "the future is in the living room," where people gather for theological reflection, dialogue, relationship, hope, information, energized action, and support.

A time to embrace the messiness of these in-between times as we strive to connect consciousness and conscience, process and action, in a free and fluid way.

A time to discover a cosmology that provides a context for personal, social, and ecological change.

A time to ponder what the divine is inviting us to create.

A time to ingest the New Universe Story, with its mystery and emergence, calling us to a fuller and greater life that is functional and inclusive.

A time to engage in the "shattering process" of a paradigm shift that summons us to experience the death of the "Clockwork God."

A time to risk being on the margins of institutions and at the center of the issues that are critical for this moment.

A time to move beyond fear, to foster a new synthesis whereby we see a new cosmology that places us at the center of human suffering.

A time to discern and discuss through dialogue and silence where the new frontiers and challenges are in each of our lives.

A time for a creativity that can heal the hole in our troubled hearts as we live through the dark night of our cultural soul.

A time to replace bullets with crayons and paintbrushes.

A time for a creativity that fosters a wholesome sexuality that leads toward a mystical union with the divine and all that is.

A time to weave together the social and ecological gospels.

A time to celebrate and always be open to surprise.

A time to explore and experience the key components of a living cosmology through a dynamic integration of geo-justice and the New Creation Story.

A time to fashion a life-affirming planetary spirituality that is mystical, prophetic, and transformative.

A time to engage in the inward journey of personal change and the outward adventure of creativity and compassion.

A time to focus on an integration of mind and body, science and spirituality, and the cognitive and experiential.

A time to become empowered by a new literacy, a shared dream experience, and story that will reveal our role in the "Great Work": the inauguration of a new era of well-being for the Earth community.

A time to ingest a planetary spirituality that evokes passion and hope; a spirituality that asks us to grow our hearts, so that they may be more open to beauty as we fashion a new world order that is sensitive, compassionate, and just.

A time for a new global ethic that moves us away from a culture of consumption, competition, and control.

A time to articulate a planetary spirituality to meet the challenges of transforming the world.

A time to celebrate a planetary spirituality that reveals our deeper destiny, embraces the new creation story, honors geo-justice making, is rooted in an expanded vision of our traditions, and fosters intimacy and energy for the soul.

What is hope? It is the presentiment that imagination is more real and reality less real than it looks. It is the hunch that the overwhelming brutality of facts that oppress and repress is not the last word. It is the suspicion that Reality is more complex than realism wants us to believe, that the frontiers of the possible are not determined by the limits of the actual, and that in a miraculous and unexpected way, life is preparing the creative events which will open the way to freedom and resurrection.

Suffering and hope live from each other. Suffering without hope produces resentment and despair. Hope without suffering creates illusions, naiveté, and drunkenness.

Let us plant dates, even though those who plant them will never eat them.... We must live by the love of what we will never see. This is the secret discipline. It is a refusal to let the creative act be dissolved away in immediate sense experience, and a stubborn commitment to the future of our grandchildren. Such disciplined love is what has given prophets, revolutionaries, and saints the courage to die for the future they envisaged. They make their own bodies the seed of their highest hope.

—Rubem Alves

THE INTEGRAL PROCESS

Everywhere around the globe a planetary spirituality movement is transforming the psyches and structure of the Earth community. A movement is being born; people are coming together to share their visions, empower each other, and transform their lives. People are beginning to make explicit a network of action on behalf of Earth and every species.

As a result, new programs, leaders, and communities are being discovered; new structures are being developed and new lifestyles formed.

Through "new flights of the social imagination," we are discovering where society is heading. One indication of these new directions is a renewed sensitivity to human needs and a responsiveness to all creation. Participants demonstrate interdependence, open communication, a sense of tradition, and a capacity to embrace the present movement, being stronger for their struggle and energized by expressions of hope and creativity.

In their lives, these people of the movement demonstrate the words of Stephen Tipton, "There is a hunger for a moral and social vision — there's a terribly noble idealism in people."

Seeing

~ How do you experience eruptions of new ideas, cultural events, and movements in the culture?

~ What movements have you and your friends been part of in the past? What movements are you engaged with at the moment?

~ How do you see the new cosmology energizing a movement that will bring us into the future?

Judging

~ As you observe the stirrings of the spirit that hover over our culture to evoke the dawn of a new society and a new day:

~ What do you see, feel, and experience?

~ What do you know about this resurgence in the culture?

~ What more do you need to discover to respond to this critical moment in our history?

Acting

~ Are you prepared to gather in groups of four to eight people to reflect together on the questions and process you have just experienced?

~ How do you feel called at this time to heal humanity and restore the beauty of creation?

~ What impulses call you to share planetary spirituality with others?

~ What additional work do you and your group feel called upon to undertake as you continue the process?

~ What is your interpretation of the appropriate actions for you and your colleagues in order to energize the dawning of the movement emerging in our midst?

~ Complete this phrase: "I would like to be remembered for...." Share your phrase with the group at the conclusion of the meeting.

The joys and hopes, the grief and the anxieties of the people of this age, especially those who are poor or in any way afflicted, there too are the joys and hopes, the grief and anxieties of the followers of Christ. — *Gaudium et Spes,* Vatican Council II

Conclusion

We truly need a new foundational experience, a new spirituality that would make possible a unique astonishing new recognition of all our dimensions with the vast diversity of our planetary, cosmic, historic, spiritual and transcendent reality.

—LEONARDO BOFF

THE PRINCIPLES OF A PLANETARY SPIRITUALITY

~ The New Creation Story is the context and origin point of a planetary spirituality.

~ Our cosmology reveals that everything is interconnected and diverse and has its own unique personality.

~ Earth, art, and spirit are integral dimensions of a planetary spirituality.

~ Wisdom resides in the capacity for a listening heart.

~ A sacred impulse responds to and guides our sensitivity to the divine creative energy that permeates all of life.

~ Each person has a particular call and place in the Great Work of our generation.

~ The New Creation Story's participation in a dynamic integration with the patterns of the culture will result in new relationships of harmony, balance, and peace that can be named "geo-justice."

~ The body of the person and the body of Earth are mandalas of divine wisdom and the source of truth and right-relationship.

~ There is a planetary spirituality operative in each member of the Earth community as we evolve toward meaning, purpose, and fulfillment.

~ A planetary spirituality fosters articulation of a language of the soul that amplifies our capacity to experience and express intuition, perception, movement, music, intimacy, silence, symbol, image, art, ritual, and contemplation.

~ A planetary spirituality enhances our capacity to savor each moment of existence as sacred and revelatory.

~ A planetary spirituality will be guided by a trinitarian cosmology, whereby Differentiation is understood as Creator, Interiority as Word, and Communion as Spirit.

~ A planetary spirituality is open to the wisdom of yesterday as we ponder the challenges of today and look to tomorrow with hope.

We are called to new ways of honoring the most profound aspirations of the heart. This spirituality will give new expression, meaning, and focus to joys and anxieties of the human condition. As we strive for a new planetary spirituality that is both personal (psychospiritual) and planetary (cosmic), our task will be to foster the most profound experiences of the soul. Cardinal Joseph Cardijn wrote:

> We are in a new age, a turning point — it is only clear that in the transformation of the world as it is today, all humanity is called to assume responsibility that it has never known in the past.

Afterword

by Ursula King

The Sacred Impulse is a celebration of life, of the Earth, of the joy of existence. Its words and vision embrace and affirm us by disclosing the subtle strength of a concretely rooted, realistic spirituality that nourishes and transforms. In simple, captivating words, Jim Conlon has presented to us the emerging vision of the New Universe Story, which invites and makes possible a newly emerging, strongly life-affirming and life-transforming spirituality.

It is a tremendously energizing vision that nourishes human hope and promises justice for all creation. It is a spirituality deeply rooted in a Christian vision of a sacramental cosmos and the belief that human co-creativity takes a responsible part in the ongoing act of creation. It is a spirituality that is both old and new. It is prophetic and mystical, and transformative of all human experiences. Its power challenges and invites us to greater openness and adventure, making possible life-enhancing hope and practical justice for our Earth community.

The impulse that affirms is the impulse of the spirit that gives us breath and life. But it is a concretely embodied spirit that animates all the crevices of the Earth, the bones and blood of our bodies, the patterns of our relationships and structures of our institutions, the hopes and struggles of our Earth community. This is a book full of hope because it celebrates the exaltation of all existence. It movingly tells us of the presence and power of the spirit in all life forms, a spirit that energizes and draws us forward in our human journey toward truer, fuller being by strongly connecting us to our roots in the Earth, to our bodies full of energy and strength, and to a greater, healing vision of a common cosmic destiny.

Bibliography

Adrienne, Carol. *The Purpose of Your Life.* New York: William Morrow, Eagle Books, 1998.

Anderson, Walter Truett. *The Future of the Self: Inventing the Postmodern Person.* New York: Jeremy P. Tarcher/Putnam, 1997.

Berry, Thomas. *Creative Energy: Bearing Witness for the Earth.* San Francisco: Sierra Club Books, 1988.

———. *The Dream of the Earth.* San Francisco: Sierra Club Books, 1988.

———. *Befriending the Earth: A Theology of Reconciliation between Humans and the Earth.* Mystic, Conn.: Twenty-Third Publications, 1991.

———. *Religions of India: Hinduism, Yoga, Buddhism.* Chambersburg, Pa.: Anima Publications, 1992.

———. *The Great Work: Our Way into the Future.* New York: Bell Tower, 1999.

Boff, Leonardo. *Cry of the Earth, Cry of the Poor.* Maryknoll, N.Y.: Orbis Books, 1997.

Brockelman, Paul. *Cosmology and Creation: The Spiritual Significance of Contemporary Cosmology.* New York: Oxford University Press, 1999.

Cardenal, Ernesto. *Abide in Love.* Maryknoll, N.Y.: Orbis Books, 1995.

Conlon, James. *Geo-Justice: A Preferential Option for the Earth.* San Jose, Calif.: Resource Publications, 1990.

———. *Earth Story, Sacred Story.* Mystic, Conn.: Twenty-Third Publications, 1994.

———. *Lyrics for Re-Creation: Language for the Music of the Universe.* New York: Continuum, 1997.

———. *Ponderings from the Precipice: Soulwork for the New Millennium.* Leavenworth, Kans.: Forest of Peace Publishing, 1998.

Coupland, Douglas. 1991. *Generation X: Tales for an Accelerated Culture.* New York: St. Martin's Press, 1991.

Doering, Bernard, ed. *The Philosopher and the Provocateur: The Correspondence of Jacques Maritain and Saul Alinsky.* Notre Dame, Ind.: University of Notre Dame Press, 1994.

Dupleix, André. *Fifteen Days of Prayer with Pierre Teilhard de Chardin.* Liguori, Mo.: Liguori, 1999.

Ebert, John David. *Twilight of the Clockwork God.* Tulsa, Okla.: Council Oak Books, 1999.

Feldman, Ron. *Fundamentals of Jewish Mysticism and Kabbalah.* Freedom, Calif.: Crossing Press, 1999.

Fox, Warwick. *Toward a Transpersonal Ecology: Developing New Foundations for Environmentalism.* Boston: Shambhala Publications, 1990.

Freire, Paulo. *Pedagogy of Freedom: Ethics, Democracy, and Civic Courage.* New York: Rowman & Littlefield Publishers, 1998.

Fritsch, Albert J. *Renew the Face of the Earth.* Chicago: Loyola University Press, 1987.

Gebara, Ivone. *Longing for Running Water: Ecofeminism and Liberation.* Minneapolis: Augsburg Fortress, 1999.

Grof, Stanislav. *The Cosmic Game: Explorations of the Frontiers of Human Consciousness.* Albany: State University of New York Press, 1998.

Hanh, Thich Nhat. *Going Home: Jesus and Buddha as Brothers.* New York: Riverhead Books, 1987.

Haught, John F. *God after Darwin: A Theology of Evolution.* Boulder, Colo.: Westview Press, 2000.

Hennelly, Alfred T. *Liberation Theologies: The Global Pursuit of Justice.* Mystic, Conn.: Twenty-Third Publications, 1995.

Hessel, Dieter, and Rosemary Radford Ruether, eds. *Christianity and Ecology.* Cambridge: Harvard University Press, 2000.

Heyneman, Martha. *The Breathing Cathedral: Feeling Our Way into a Living Cosmos.* San Francisco: Sierra Club, 1993.

Hill, Brennan R. *Christian Faith and the Environment.* Maryknoll, N.Y.: Orbis Books, 1998.

Horton, Myles, and Paulo Freire. *We Make the Road by Walking: Conversations on Education and Social Change.* Ed. Brenda Bell, John Gaventa, and John Peters. Philadelphia: Temple University Press, 1990.

Hull, Fritz, ed. *Earth and Spirit: The Spiritual Dimension of the Environmental Crisis*. New York: Continuum, 1993.

Johnson, Elizabeth A. *Friends of God and Prophets: A Feminist Theological Reading of the Communion of Saints*. New York: Continuum, 1998.

Kelly, Tony. *An Expanding Theology: Faith in a World of Connections*. Sydney: E. J. Dwyer, 1993.

King, Ursula. *Spirit of Fire: The Life and Vision of Teilhard de Chardin*. Maryknoll, N.Y.: Orbis Books, 1996.

———. *Christ in All Things: Exploring Spirituality with Teilhard de Chardin*. Maryknoll, N.Y.: Orbis Books, 1997.

———. *Pierre Teilhard de Chardin*. Maryknoll, N.Y.: Orbis Books, 1999.

Lesser, Elizabeth. *The New American Spirituality: A Seeker's Guide*. New York: Random House, 1999.

Liebes, Sidney, Elisabet Sahtouris, and Brian Swimme. *A Walk in Time: From Stardust to Us*. New York: John Wiley & Sons, 1998.

MacKinnon, Mary Heather, and Moni McIntyre, eds. *Readings in Ecology and Feminist Theology*. Kansas City: Sheed & Ward, 1995.

Macy, Joanna, and Molly Young Brown. *Coming Back to Life: Practices to Reconnect Our Lives, Our World*. Stony Creek, Conn.: New Society Publishers, 1998.

McFague, Sallie. *The Body of God: An Ecological Theology*. Minneapolis: Fortress Press, 1993.

———. *Super, Natural Christians: How We Should Love Nature*. Minneapolis: Fortress Press, 1997.

McGuinnes, Mary, and Miriam Therese MacGillis. *Our Origin Story*. Plainfield, N.J.: Renew International, 1999.

Merton, Thomas. *Contemplation in a World of Action*. Notre Dame, Ind.: University of Notre Dame Press, 1998.

Moore, Thomas. *Original Self: Living with Paradox and Originality*. New York: HarperCollins, 2000.

O'Donohue, John. *Anam Cara: A Book of Celtic Wisdom*. New York: HarperCollins, Cliff Street Books, 1997.

———. *Eternal Echoes: Exploring Our Yearning to Belong*. New York: HarperCollins, Cliff Street Books, 1999.

Oliver, Mary. *New and Selected Poems*. Boston: Beacon Press, 1992.

O'Murchu, Diarmuid. *Quantum Theology: Spiritual Implications of the New Physics*. New York: Crossroad, 1998.

———. *Reclaiming Spirituality: A New Spiritual Framework for Today's World*. New York: Crossroad, 1998.

———. *Poverty, Celibacy, and Obedience: A Radical Option for Life*. New York: Crossroad, 1999.

———. *Religion in Exile: A Spiritual Homecoming*. New York: Crossroad, 1999.

O'Sullivan, Edmund. *Transformative Learning: Educational Vision for the Twenty-First Century*. New York: Zed Books, 1999.

Palmer, Parker. *Let Your Life Speak: Listening for the Voice of Vocation*. San Francisco: Jossey-Bass Publishers, 2000.

Roberts, Elizabeth, and Elias Amidon, eds. *Earth Prayers*. San Francisco: HarperSanFrancisco, 1991.

Ruether, Rosemary Radford. *Gaia and God: An Ecofeminist Theology of Earth Healing*. San Francisco: HarperSanFrancisco, 1992.

———. *Women Healing Earth: Third World Women on Ecology, Feminism, and Religion*. Maryknoll, N.Y.: Orbis Books, 1996.

Scharper, Stephen Bede. *Redeeming the Time: A Political Theology of the Environment*. New York: Continuum, 1997.

Shea, John. *Gospel Light: Jesus Stories for Spiritual Consciousness*. New York: Crossroad, 1998.

Somé, Malidoma Patrice. *The Healing Wisdom of Africa: Finding Life Purpose through Nature, Ritual, and Community*. New York: Putnam, 1999.

Steindl-Rast, David. *A Listening Heart*. New York: Crossroad, 2000.

Swimme, Brian, and Thomas Berry. *The Universe Story*. San Francisco: HarperSanFrancisco, 1992.

Swindells, John, ed. *A Human Search: Bede Griffiths Reflects on His Life*. Liguori, Mo.: Triumph Books, 1997.

Teilhard de Chardin, Pierre. *Man's Place in Nature: The Human Zoological Group*. New York: Harper Colophon Books, 1966.

———. *The Human Phenomenon*. Ed. and trans. Sarah Appleton-Weber. Portland, Ore., and Brighton, U.K.: Sussex Academic Press, 1999.

Wallis, Jim. *The Soul of Politics*. Maryknoll, N.Y.: Orbis Books, 1994.

Webb, Benjamin. *Fugitive Faith: Conversations on Spiritual, Environmental, and Community Renewal.* Maryknoll, N.Y.: Orbis Books, 1998.

Wheatley, Margaret. *Leadership and the New Science: Learning about Organization from an Orderly Universe.* San Francisco: Berrett-Koehler Publishers, 1992.

Whyte, David. *The House of Belonging.* Langley, Wash.: Many Rivers Press, 1997.

Winter, Miriam Therese. *The Singer and the Song: An Autobiography of the Spirit.* Maryknoll, N.Y.: Orbis Books, 1999.